Anonymus

An old Englishman's opinion on Schleswig-Holstein and Germany

Being a practical evidence for the justice of their cause, given after a 50 years'

residence in Germany

Anonymus

An old Englishman's opinion on Schleswig-Holstein and Germany
*Being a practical evidence for the justice of their cause, given after a 50 years'
residence in Germany*

ISBN/EAN: 9783743336230

Manufactured in Europe, USA, Canada, Australia, Japa

Cover: Foto ©ninafisch / pixelio.de

Manufactured and distributed by brebook publishing software
(www.brebook.com)

Anonymus

An old Englishman's opinion on Schleswig-Holstein and Germany

AN OLD ENGLISHMAN'S

OPINION

ON

Schleswig-Holstein

AND

Germany,

being a practical Evidence for the Justice of their cause,
given after a 50 years' residence in Germany.

WITH SUPPLEMENT OF OFFICIAL DOCUMENTS.

A non-official Blue-Book,

DEDICATED TO EVERY ONE OF THE AUTHOR'S COUNTRYMEN,
as a Testimony of hearty Acknowledgment for the German Nation.

"Nullos mortalium *armis* aut *fide* ante Germanos esse."
(The German Chieftains, of the Frisick tribe, in Rome, 59 after Christ.)

LONDON, 1864.
TRÜBNER & CO., 60 Paternoster Row.

Printed as a Manuscript for those immediately Concerned.

Price 6 d. for sale. N.B.— The entire Proceeds to be devoted:
One half to the Danish wounded, and
The other half to the War-sufferers in Schleswig.

Introduction.

Motto: Don't deny Fair play, but do as you'd be done by.

ENGLISHMEN,

In that small and despised Schleswig-Holstein not only the *Honour*, but likewise the most vital *Interests of our country are at stake!* Let therefore every fair-thinking man, as well as every tax-payer, &c., give me an earnest hearing—for **L., s.** and **d.** are deeply involved.

Much has been written about this once so-called "Storm in a tea-pot," which quickly baffled all English calculations—a decisive proof that it never was understood. **If you want to know what a thoroughly independent Englishman has to say about it:** then read this short pamphlet. You may at the same time find out, that **this same Schleswig-Holstein affair is a handle to the most important Events in Europe**...

What would you say, if it *could* be proved that the Liberation of Schleswig-Holstein is nothing more than the natural developement of a just and legitimate cause?! which possesses even greater merits than Hungary and Poland, if you were to find that the real well-being of Denmark is by no means injured in consequence;—and what, if finally you were to discover that at the same time the Interests of our country will strongly gain thereby?!

I will tell you then, that this most desirable supposition—is *the actual Reality*. I'll pledge you my honour to the correctness of the Facts, which I give partly from my own long Experience on the spot, partly from the most independent sources, and therefore undeniable, except, possibly, in immaterial particulars.

As soon as you examine *independently*, instead of being swayed by a "gregarious" public opinion, founded on one-sided *reports:* you will discover that most of the *dangers* which alarm you— *are of your own creation*. For it is the English Government that has permitted Denmark to decide upon an unjust and self-destructive *invasion of German rights;* it is the English Government like-wise, that has done all in its power to *kindle a general war!*

Extreme contradictions of truth may be brought on by delusive outside-appearances, in-rooted by ruling opinion:—on this very day the Italians celebrate the 300th anniversary of one of their greatest men, but who was persecuted as a Heretic during his life-time for declaring that our Earth does not stand still (!). I mean *Galilei* (2 months the senior of our Shakespeare). Extremes often meet, that is an established fact—and the Schleswig-Holstein case offers the newest illustration. Since that great age of general Reformation, however, the *"Move-on"* principle most decidedly governs, sweeping before it all resistance. If you look the time-present boldly in the face, the imagined dangers will disappear like a Nightmare. Providence has acted more kindly for us than we ourselves, by upsetting that short-sighted "London-Protocol." We have little more to do than give up interfering with *a natural developement*—the consequences will then most assuredly give us reason to rejoice.

Anyhow, my Countrymen, I felt it a most urgent Duty to speak out *my sincere Convictions!*

(*18th February.*)

⟶⟶ Postscript ⟵⟵

This *Explanation* has been **denied publishment in England!** by one of my oldest friends—from whose liberal principles I had expected a cheerful assistance to the *rescue* of a cause simply *conservative.*

Such *One-sidedness* has added a spur, to overhaul and extend, and to add some weighty documentary Vouchers, which have come into my possession.

I hail with greatest satisfaction the co-operation of a *Nobleman* like Sir Francis Head! Yes, indeed, passions must be set aside, nothing save a cool, thorough investigation of the Root of the Wound—although momentarily painful—can enable a permanent cure (for which I offer some Suggestions).

Such investigation I shall attempt, with equity and candour for *all* parts. My peculiar position may enable me to assist like an *Interpreter.* And let the Critics recollect that I do not pretend to more than a practical conviction, and that I am a *Non-professional.*

France is ahead of us at present—shall we delay giving a casting vote for the just cause of Schleswigholstein?—thus establishing new Guarantees for the peace and well-being of Europe, and for the Glory of our Country!

An old Englishman.

Hamburg, 23rd April, 1864.

I.

ENGLAND *versus* SCHLESWIG-HOLSTEIN!

"The Channel-Fleet and 20—30,000 English soldiers are to be sent forthwith to assist our Remonstrations against an Invasion of Denmark by the Germans (who attempt to seize two of the best Danish Provinces), or eventually for the Fulfilment of our Guarantee-obligations. The Commander-in-chief is already appointed."—*Morning Post* and *Daily News* of 28th January, 1864.

Such is the language sent into the world by English papers.— Now the Englishmen of the present day are not the Englishmen of 1775, when the Hotspur-aristocracy of the nation would not listen to the calm and most reasonable argument made by their brethren of North-America, who were in a high degree tyrannised and oppressed. And even when their famous delegate Benjamin Franklin, who was so warm in England's cause, was sent to plead at the Bar of the House, he would not be listened to, but had to fly to France where a ready hand was lent to the Americans. And so was one of the finest Colonies lost to England for ever, by cause of tyranny and oppression. The only portion which remains (Canada), allowed to govern itself, is for this reason a contented and loyal country. England has from that time had the wisdom to treat all its growing colonies in the same manner, retaining only a certain protectorate. From that day to the present has England made great advances in political civilisation, and, to do it credit, has used every nerve to further commerce and the interchange of national commodities, that war might be severed from the fate of nations, especially of Europe.

But in the case of Schleswig-Holstein I see the English in danger of committing a most flagrant contradiction against their own vital principles, and which would undoubtedly fall back on their own heads. An unjust prejudice rules public opinion against

1

Germany, probably owing to the activity of the adversary reporters. But is this excusable? since an excessive considerate regard for peace is a proverbial quality of the Germans, and history records how oft' they have had to pay the piper.—England sadly needs Information on *the facts,* and to alter her course accordingly; otherwise a most unexpected Crisis may be brought on.—Beware and reconsider your Verdict!

For what should English troops be sent to engage in a war to which there may be no end known? Are you aware, Englishmen, that the sailing and marching of such a force would cost the country ten times more than the supporting of the unemployed operatives caused by the Cotton-famine? that the stroke is aimed at your own best customers in commerce?—And may it not be justly said that the almost entire blame of this war may be put on England's shoulders!—

It is to uphold the **London Treaty,** the Integrity of Denmark, the Balance of power, they say, that the English speak so loud. But who was the father of this Protocol? Why, *Russia* that put forward England and a few other great nations to stand godfathers.—The intention may have been good enough—for Russia (!); we would have found that out soon enough in case it had ever come into binding force! But the English public appear to be so much in the dark as not to know that the primary conditions of the meditated new arrangement have never been fulfilled, and that therefore said Protocol has never been more than so much waste paper. The most learned lawyers and statesmen have proved this. England is only in the position of a man who has put his signature to the will of a friend, as a Witness. It proves that an Estate has been therein disposed of, which never belonged to deceased. Can the Witnesses be called upon to assist in purloining the property from the lawful heir?! Germany has never sanctioned the dismemberment of her territory, the family of the legal Heir have never abdicated, * and, above all, *the parliamentary Repre-*

---

* The senior Duke of Augustenburg, on receiving at last about one-half the value of his personal Estates, merely promised (under constraint) "not in any way to oppose the resolutions which H. M. (of Denmark) may have taken, or in future might take, neither in reference to the order of succession to all the lands now united under H. M.'s sceptre, nor as to the eventual organisation of H. M.'s monarchy."

sentatives of Schleswig-Holstein have never consented; nay, the chance was not even given to them—they were actually never asked.— I shall have occasion to take up this subject once more (page 15) with some most important hints.

A clear starting point must first be gained in order to understand the *present* state of things. The English public and even the ministry are partly behind the time, they mix what is passed with the present. The preceding King of Denmark *was* by legal claim likewise Duke of Schleswig-Holstein; with him by mutual consent new arrangements *might* have been made; if he had not broken the peace-treaty of 51, things *might* have taken a different turn. But death cut him off as a *refractory* Liegeman, and Germany has now to do *only* with his legal successor Frederick VIII. "This is a necessary consequence of the primitive conventions of historical right," as Baron von Geiger, in his speech in the French Legislative Assembly of 31st January, clearly proved.

To debate about the **Integrity of Denmark** is a mere humbug (or something worse), for nobody either questions or threatens it. The position of Schleswig-Holstein exactly corresponded with that of Hanover up to 1837, viz., that of perfect Independence and only a *dynastic* union. *Holstein*—as even Denmark does not deny—*is an integral part of Germany,* and it possesses an *"undividable connection for ever" with Schleswig,* which condition likewise has been acknowledged by oath by each successive King-Duke. *Schleswig,* having been for 500 years—by charter, interest, and nationality—amalgamated with a German province (and *not* being a part of Denmark), is therefore to all intents and purposes *a part of Germany.* The Prussian province of Prussia-proper stands in a position exactly corresponding. Both are not formally classed as members of the German Empire, owing to its loose organisation and long distraction.

As to an alteration of the **Balance of power** through restoring Schleswig-Holstein to the German Confederation,—or in other words to a connexion very little more intimate than that which Belgium has to France—can anybody who knows the circumstances raise such an assertion without blushing?! For almost every nation of Europe has in possession a piece of Germany!;

1 *

even England holds Helgoland.*—Germany was seriously injured
by the Danish connection with Schleswig-Holstein. Only during
the last general war Denmark aided and fought against Germany.

Who begins *this broil* which is lighting up Europe as it were
in a flame? Not the Germans, but *the Danes.* After tyrannising
over Schleswig-Holstein to the utmost, after an unparalleled long-
suffering on the part of Germany, the Danes—adding insult to
breach of all faith—incorporated Schleswig, which was a deadly
affront. Danish garrisons in Schleswig-Holstein (never legal) had
become equal to an invading army of enemies after death had
separated the only connexion of personal union between the two
independent countries. I'll venture to say that no other nation,
save Germany through its melancholy disunion. would or could
have waited one fortnight before enforcing its rights. But Germany
actually let the splendid opportunity escape when frost had built .
a bridge for their army to take the formidable Dannewerke com
paratively easy!

Now there were many feelers sent out before the Danes had the
audacity to take away Schleswig. As to the Germans, they pronounced protests against the idea, but were not heeded. Englishmen, ye boasted lovers of liberty and fair play, why was not your
voice heard? You sent special Envoys over probably instead of
dispatches. They may have all been very well-meaning; but it
would have been more manly on your part to have dealt openly
before the world with the Danes—as you did in your official notes
to Germany.—We may even without any bad intention say that
England has perhaps done Denmark more harm than Germany
ever can. For the Germans are only fulfilling one part of their
national rights, by protecting what is their own—and at the last
extremity of danger. I was not referring to direct deeds of hosti-
lity, but to the treaty of Vienna. I think Castlereagh there played
a very conspicuous part, and England must have been a very bad
friend of Denmark, being a party in **tearing off Norway,** and
only giving in recompense another *German* (!) province: Lauenburg,

---

* Highly pleasing and eloquent is the contrast of happiness evinced by these
Schleswig-Holstein islanders under *our* protection. And their late resolution for
this reason deserves double credit, viz., to deny pilotage to any danish war-craft.

from which they could not march any soldiers, only taking away a small yearly revenue. And now comes the curse of that same Vienna congress, splitting nations, seeking to destroy nationalities which would for ever keep the world in a fermenting state. So they took Finland from Sweden, with what right? And to this day are the Finlanders contemplating an uprise against the Russians to get free from foreign power, although the present honourable Emperor is restoring their prerogatives. Look at Greece, Belgium, Italy, Poland, and Greece *second*-edition (which England has favoured in glaring contradiction to Schleswig-Holstein), &c., &c.—a dozen of unnatural treaties riddled!—England could not *conquer* the Scotch, and yet they are the most loyal people of the island. How different the case with conquered Ireland! The Swedes exercise very little dominion over the Norwegians, who are wise enough to be governed according to their ancient laws, and to admit of no Swedes among them. Certainly every country has sufficient of its own population to place in offices. Thus where the nationalities are respected, how different the result.

But what is most, ye Englishmen, that you should think about, is that there is some one over the water very well prepared to make a great political move on any political error, which should get England well edged into a war, and to carry on which war it would require at least a 100,000 soldiers. With all her boast of strength probably to her own destruction; for it would be the very means to unite the great German nation, who would send millions of soldiers as good as any in the world. But what would you say; ye Englishmen, when pleased with a little splash-dash of your great big ships, you were to read of a concentration at Cherbourg of iron-clad frigates, countless gun-boats, and of troops? Would you not begin to feel a little uneasy at home, and repent when too late of the great humbug which in your folly you followed up? There is a strong war-party in France, and almost every action of their present government has so far had an ultimate aim at England. First Russia was fought and reduced with the assistance of England, and somehow an estrangement between England and Russia has continued. Then Austria was weakened, and Italy fostered as an auxiliary-dependent. And now, if England was to attack Germany, all this would be the prelude of the ultimate attempt against England. It does indeed deserve the greatest acknowledgment that France does of late prove a noble insight, by manifestations for justice and peace. But keep your eye upon *the war-party* to which my remarks apply, and which through the late measures of England has been encouraged. Witness a recent Paris correspondence of the "Herald," which deserves attention.

My advice would be:—Let knaves fight their own battles, but be you not their assistants, for there is assuredly "something rotten in the state of Denmark." Keep your watch upon your neighbour, and preserve in readiness your strength. Rely upon it, the hour is approaching when you will stand in need of it!

I'll now attempt to give some *general information,* and *evidences for the Rights* of

Schleswig-Holstein.*

The case itself is so clear,—but its confusion and distortion in England almost beyond belief!—Since you are in such a fighting humour, here are even terms: Overcome my paper "Columns" by *facts,* then I'll give in with good grace.—Reality, however, can be harangued away only temporarily. You are misled, and in a dense fog. An old Outpost-sentinel warns you: "Hold on!"—it is only just time to save you from firing at your own Friends!

The case has been *compared* by the French Minister Mr. Drouin 19th Jan.) *to* **Belgium.** Now I expect to prove that, as the claims of Belgium required fulfilment in opposition to treaty and law, those of *Schleswig-Holstein* are *doubly undeniable,* because accompanied with *legality* and yet so unfairly attacked. (Respecting Lord Cowley's denial—how can such a contradiction of *events* be explained!) Let us examine the facts, the Reality.

I will introduce "that tough old question" by translating it into English. Indeed, my *Home-illustration* is founded upon an

---

* The following is worked out by a son of mine, who, by advantages of personal observation and study since 1848, and aided by repeated visits to almost all parts of Schleswig-Holstein, surpasses me in knowledge and insight of the entire circumstances.

historical reminiscence, which appears to be growing almost fashionable and tasty (?)—viz., that our country was once "a conquered danish province."* I need perhaps not ask pardon then, for bringing before your mind the supposed case: that Denmark should continue at this day to maintain possession only of our county of Kent, and merely as a fief, a pledge of lingering old friendship.

To explain such a nonentity as even possible, I must of course further assume that the same fundamental evil of Germany *might* have befallen us, viz., the ancient misery of Heptarchy come to life again!—the Dukes and Lords of Counties, &c., upstarted as "sovereign" Kings, Dukes, &c., with some miniature "town Republics" (perhaps Hull or Liverpool) to complete the confusion. Imagine England without a fleet, without any national Parliament: in fact, merely a very loose connection by a many-minded assemblage of Government-*servants*: a Diet!

Well then, suppose the King of Denmark to be at the same time Duke of Kent. Crossing over to the south-east part of London, you would have duty to pay, enforced by Danish officials and Danish soldiers in Danish coin; you would see Danish colours flying all along that side of the Thames-river, and perhaps a Danish man-of-war here or there moored. On a visit to Copenhagen you would meet your Kent countrymen doing duty at King Christian's palace, officered by foreigners, commanded in Danish. Would any Englishman find consolation by "arguments" of close blood-relationship between the respective royal famlilies?!—And if, to conclude the analogy—after 400 years of troubles—such a revolting guardianship were at last dissolved, and in a fully legal manner, like a very Godsend,--what would you say and do if France interfered, upraiding you for the pettyness of your complaints; charging you with oppressing and plundering cowardly so small a power, &c., &c.; and if she finally went a begging to all the powers, for a general razzia against England!

Putting your foot out of this City, you step into Altona, which

---

* Let me only remind you of the "Alexandra-Vase," which is crowned by "a statuette of Canute, the Royal Anglo-Dane, with his crown and sceptre and mantle of state, as he might have appeared when he rose from his chair beside the advancing waters of the flowing tide." (!)—*Illustr. London News.*

is naturally a component part of Hamburg, but cut off by foreigners; all the northern side of the river Elbe—the Thames of Germany— has been in Danish hands for centuries. Instead of overdoing, my sketch is drawn only in pale colours. If you knew the Schleswig-Holstein case, you would be astounded at the awful carricature, and disgusted, no doubt, at the prominent part therein taken by our country!—But to proceed with *facts:*

Schleswig-Holstein is *a* **distinct** *and* **independent** *country,* composed of 2 Duchies united "for ever undividable" (formerly usually comprised under the name simply of *Holstein,* or the *German* Duchies [provinces, lands] of the King-Duke). At the dawn of history (after the Cimbrians had issued forth from this peninsula to the terror of Rome) the *German* Anglo-Saxons and Frisians appear to have inhabited not only all S.-Holstein, but likewise a considerable part of present Jutland. Some centuries later the *Scandinavian* Normans, in particular the Danes (whose original home-country was in their Islands and southern Sweden), commenced their inroads—being much aided by the large emigration which had left the country in the preceding period for England, * which wholesale emigrations appear to have been originally induced by most awful Flood-devastations† (for in all probability the Atlantic then broke through the Channel and cut off England as an island). The struggles between Scandinavians and Germans continued for centuries with varying success, and war followed after war. The Danes conquered Jutland (which was a Germanic country) in 863, also many other parts of northern

---

* For an intelligent Englishman there cannot be a more interesting neighbour-hood than those parts of Schleswig-Holstein which have maintained a very great portion of our Forefathers' distinguishing characteristics. I allude to the venerable remains of the ancient Anglo-Saxon (Frisick) shore, which have preserved character by having been cut off from the main-land and insulated. Let me name the island of *Sylt* where you are still shown the port whence Hengist and Horsa departed! You are greeted in a dialect resembling that in which our great Alfred wrote:— "Good e'en, good dai." You find a sturdy serious population of regular tars, bear-ing the same stamp as ours. Churches are pointed out to you as built by Willi-brord or other Missionaries from the Island-colony. (And by-the-bye, these same Sylters, although at the mercy of the enemy's war-ships, have maintained well their heroic patriotism. At life risk their deputation, for the acknowledgment of Duke Frederick, passed through the icy seas, &c. And just now the news comes in of their having taken prisoners some Danish marines sent to seize their public moules.)

† See Dr. von Maack's highly interesting treatise:—"*Das urgeschichtliche Schles-wig-Holstein.*"

Germany were long troubled, and for times partially in their possession. Particularly the north-eastern division of the border Duchy of Schleswig was seriously visited by them; the Jutlanders, &c., pressing forward into the evacuated parts, and for a long time the Danes treated Schleswig as a Liege-country. But at other times German influence ruled over the whole of Jutland as well as over the Kingdom of the Danes—their crown being more than once conferred, as a sort of dependancy, by the Emperors of Germany.

At last the year 1326 brought about a clear settlement: the cession of Schleswig to the German Duchy of Holstein as a hereditary fief under the express stipulation (Constitution of Waldemar III.) that Denmark should nevermore undertake an incorporation of Schleswig; and this was confirmed by the Danish "Rigsraad." New aggressions took place; but in a decisive war - of 20 years' duration—Schleswig-Holstein in 1435 most triumphantly maintained her rights against Denmark, which at that time possessed Sweden and Norway. Indeed, Schleswig-Holstein was so much in the ascendancy, that 13 years later the throne of Denmark was offered to Count Adolphus VIII. of Schleswig-Holstein. *He refused it*, but by his recommendation his nephew Christian I. (a German) was elected King of Denmark.

Unfortunately that noble Adolphus VIII. died without issue. Let particular attention be paid to the Arrangements then made for his succession; for in these you will find a perfect solution of the present difficulty. The intention may have been, that a permanent peaceable *Alliance* be brought about between Schleswig-Holstein and her ambitious neighbour *by uniting the respective crowns on one head* (although at the same time some intrigues co-operated to set aside another relative of the deceased). Anyhow, it supplies a strong proof for the power of the people's Representatives that, not by decree or treaty, but *by their sovereign vote*, the ducal Crown of Schleswig-Holstein was entrusted to the King of Denmark, under the strictest conditions of Independence and Charter-rights. All the present quibbles are as it were foreseen, and struck down flat by the express words with which the King-Dukes of Schleswig-Holstein have sanctioned their Covenant "the Privileges of the Lands," viz.:—

"We confess (acknowledge) and attest openly by these presents, that the Re-
"presentatives of Schleswig and Holstein (as particularly described) have elected
"Us to be their Duke; likewise have the aforenamed accepted us and rendered
"homage to us as their sovereign, *not as a King of Denmark*, but as their Lord
"over the aforedescribed Lands, &c."

And again:—

"being elected, not as a King of Denmark, but by the favour which the in-
"habitants possess for our person: these Lands shall not be by Us bequeathed
"to one of our childen or relatives, but after our decease,—inasmuch as We
"are now chosen by free will of the inhabitants: so shall they and their off-
"spring as often as the throne become vacant: continue to exercise their right
"of choosing for their Lord one of our children or heirs, &c.

Also further providing for the contingencies possible at a new
ducal Election:—

"and the (new) Duke shall be bounden to newly confirm, meliorate, &c., and
"to swear to all the Privileges given and confirmed by Us. *If he should, how-
"ever, refuse, then the Inhabitants shall be freed from any obligation to elect that
"same King their Lord*, but shall then choose one of Our nearest Heirs."

This right of special election was likewise occasionally made use
of until 1650, when primogeniture was introduced, bnt with the
special condition acknowledging only *male*-succession, in contradiction to the Danish law where females are admitted.

Painful to relate that generous trust and faith proved an almost
deadly mistake. For while the vows of the royal Dukes, repeated
at every accession, half lulled the people to rest, and the cotem-
porary great wars distracted them: almost unperceived, because
slowly and piecemeal, *the rights of Schleswig-Holstein were gradually
injured.* Their parliament (last sitting 1712), independant flag and
army, right of exclusive native officials, and likewise of separate
peace and war, were one by one escamoteed. The country was
even parcelled out as domains for the junior branches of the
sovereign-family. Quarrels and even wars ensued in consequence,
in which Sweden took part against Denmark. From such an internal struggle between two family members about one part of
Schleswig sprung that *so-called* Guarantee of 1720, which was merely
a confirmation of a change of hands by force, and never dreamt
to interfere with the Independance, &c., of Schleswig-Holstein, as
the Dispatches of George II. prove expressly. Here then is another
Bugbear exploded!—to the relief of Lord Shaftesbury.—Gradually
Schleswig-Holstein was depressed and treated more like a feeding
province for the ruling party in Denmark.

The fact is, Schleswig-Holstein never was secure against her stronger neighbour. Nor could there ever exist a lasting harmony between these two *nationalities,* because they are so *strongly opposed:* The Anglo-Frisick *Saxons* of Schleswig-Holstein have maintained their brave tenacious love of liberty and their somewhat blunt innate goodness (which qualities they so successfully transplanted to Angl'-island * [Angleterre-England]).—Now the *Danish* people do likewise possess a strong good-nature and patriotism. (Indeed, the Germans might learn from their patriotic energy, although at present so sadly misguided.) But the very narrow limits of their language and their out-of-the-way geographical position render them rather backward in higher cultivation and one-sided in judgment. (Look at their soldiers: as if just called from the plough.) Examining their character in history, we find them hurried on by a patriotic but excessive ambition. Thus their glory became blood-stained. It was out of all proportion that they grasped all Scandinavia, considerable parts of Germany, England, Ireland, &c., under their dominion. A strong portion of that ancient Vikinger-character has been inherited particularly by the upper classes of Danes; it hurls them into passionate excesses this very day. They possess much gallantry and polish of manners, but a strong smack of martial-law discipline, as on board ship; their own nation generally suffer thereby, not the Schleswig-Holsteiners alone. Why did our Ancestors hate them? (Think of our great King Alfred, and of the awful struggles they likewise had to overcome, for 230 years.) And why did the Swedes cast off a kindred dominion, two or three times? The Danish Kings for centuries wielded unbounded dominion. It is said that country now enjoys one of the most free constitutions; but it would appear as if the main difference were that a many share now what was formerly swayed by one hand.

The physiological explanation of the fate of the Danes may be found in their excess of ambition. Perhaps the loss of Norway influenced the present aim of the Danish leaders? viz., to "annex"

* To those acquainted with the German language I can strongly recommend a perusal of "Schleswig, the original Home of the non-danish Angelish and Frisick tribes, and the Mother-country of England; what it was and what it has come to," written by Dr. K. J. Clement (a fine old Frisian himself), and well deserving a translation.

the German provinces entrusted to their Sovereign. The Schleswig-Holsteiners in their agricultural and seafaring pursuits shared
the German peaceable disposition, and are even blameable for an
excess of loyal submission, until finally such ungrateful tyranny
grew intolerable. — — The preceding gives **a Key** *to the incessant disagreements between the Danes and Germans.* For more
than a 1000 years, in some 10 different bloody wars, and in
troubles with but short intermission Schleswig-Holstein has suffered
from Denmark. Separation is unavoidable. Both parties will gain
thereby.

Schleswig-Holstein possesses fine resources, but only somewhat
more than *one-half the population of Denmark* (900,000 against
1.600,000)! beside the disadvantages through the abuse of ruling
power. How the contemplation of this fact must turn upside down,
one of the fundamental unjust ideas established in England!
I mean that false Pity for an alleged weakness of Denmark. Perhaps you may retort:—Yes, but the superior power of all Germany?—Know then, that Germany, unable even to help itself, has
neglected Schleswig-Holstein in such a woeful manner that on the
contrary it has committed hostile acts. For, after a passing mock-
encouragement, the German Great-powers did in 1851 betray Schleswig-Holstein to Denmark. Likewise their ever signing that London
Treaty—although they did so under certain conditions—was quite
an unjust action.—You will find out presently which is the weak
and oppressed side! But read on.

For centuries the little country had stood alone, almost entirely
abandoned by its natural protector, sometimes forced to fight
against the latter (Germany), suffering its fate with excessive
patience. After Napoleon had caused the German imperial crown
to be laid down, Denmark actually attempted (in 1806) to incorporate
also the German province of Holstein, but was rebuffed, and thus
the first most loyal opposition awakened, which regained some lost
ground. But the loss of Norway (1815) appears to have been the
turning point. A party grew up who sought to acquire at least
Schleswig to prevent its falling off at the long foreseen event of
Frederick VII. dying childless. Here then it will be laid open,
who were:—

the **Originators** of the Schleswig-Holstein Difficulties?

I am enabled to do so by giving a quotation from G. L. Baden, the respected *Danish* historian's explanation, published in Berling's newspaper, No. 51, February, 1837; viz.:—

"Mr. Orla Lehmann (the head of the Eider-Dane party, and raised to be ruling Minister through that insurrection of 1848), Mr. L. acknowledges that in the Duchy of Schleswig the German 'language prevails and is the one used by all men of education, whereas—I quote his own expression—the Danish language is that of the rabble. He alleges that the German language was chiefly introduced there by church-reformation, and grants Germany at that period to have stood on a higher stage of developement than Denmark. As, however, this higher state of cultivation does still exist; as every educated man in Schleswig-Duchy speaks, writes, and reads German; and as the majority know nothing whatever of the Danish language,—I may well advance the question, whether it be fair to injure the educated class, to render them almost useless members of the state, or anyhow to reduce their value so that they may even find themselves compelled to try to leave the country,—and all this on account of the (Danish-speaking) mob?"

To which I add further extracts from the same source, viz:—

"consequently the worthy historian of Prussia, Rühs, may well be in the right, in asserting that it would be an attack upon the very life conditions of Schleswig-Holstein, if it should now be divided" *

and:—

'It is sufficient that I have drawn attention here to this, that it would be a Sin to separate Schleswig from Holstein, because such separation would destroy the prosperity of both countries."

Only in 1846, when Denmark thought the time for dismasking arrived, proclaiming by an "Open Letter" the abolishment of Charter rights and of the legitimate succession: only then Schleswig-Holstein and Germany were aroused to an understanding of the wrongful stratagem. But Denmark *retracted* once more; the King-Duke, on being called upon by Germany, expressly declared that Scheswig and Holstein were entitled to a joint legislature and administration, and that he would respect the rights of the "Agnati" (legal Heirs). Whereupon the German Diet resolved (Sept. 17, 1846) that the King-Duke must respect the rights of the States and Agnati, and reserved its competence for future decisions—*which resolution stands binding this very day.*

I quote the following from the "Memorial to Lord J. Russell by H. M. Chargé d'affaires Mr. J. Ward," dated Jan. 31, 1862, viz.:—

---

* The above proves at the same time that it is impossible to carry out one of the schemes of Lord J. Russell, which was to cut up Schleswig between Germany and Denmark; for this would literally *cut up the interests* of the whole country. The small Danish party there, most unfairly augmented, can certainly not afford a sufficient pretext.

"The (deceased) Kiug, Frederick VII., on his accession recognised
the rights of Schleswig and Holstein (as all have done!) in a Proclama-
tion dated January 28, 1848; but on March 21, 1848, *an insurrection*
of a democratic character broke out *in Copenhagen,* whose objects
were the *abolition of the Constitution* by States then in force in
Denmark as well as in *Schleswig-Holstein,* to *separate* Schleswig
from Holstein, and to *incorporate* the former with the Kingdom
of Denmark.

**"Against these revolutionary objects began the
movement in the Duchies, which was purely defensive of their rights,** and was approved in principle by
the King of Prussia. The Schleswig-Holstein cause was, in fact,
the *maintainance* of the 400 years' *union* between the two Duchies
under the King-Duke, and **their independence** of the rule
of the kingdom of Denmark Proper.

"Out of these movements arose the war between Germany and
Denmark."

One fact must be brought to light here, which speaks volumes
for the faith and character of the Schleswigholsteiners: Notwithstanding all those provocations, their movements remained purely
defensive. They never attempted to set aside the late King-Duke,
notwithstanding his fighting them for 3 years; if they did not love
him, yet they admitted some excuse on account of the party-
suppression under which he may himself have suffered.

The famous German Sham-war against the Danes was ended by
a Peace signed by Austria and Prussia, and subsequently ratified
by the (illegally) reconstituted German Diet—an "unsatisfactory
arrangement, because it did not, in fact, settle any one of the
questions which gave rise to the war." What do you say to that
small Schleswig-Holstein, ill-treated by friend and by foe, continuing never daunted to fight on alone? gallantly withstanding
and often thrashing double numbers, free from overbearing in
success, and of despondence in reverses. Denmark never conquered. The cruel end was that the German Government broke
faith, disarming 43,248 soldiers,* and then delivering over, with

* Schleswig-Holstein had nearly 6 per cent. of her population under arms,
and made such enormous sacrificies without murmuring. To Denmark were

arms, ships, stores and all, Schleswigholstein to its Hereditary-enemy!

At this point I must most impressively call attention to the Cause of the crooked unnatural course into which the Schleswig-Holstein affair was forced, and to *the possible consequences for England.* It was the Government of Czar Nicholas II., then on the culminating point of influence that coerced Prussia and the German nation to a breach of right and promises even during the war and in the peace. Recollect that he was the "protector" of the German Governments against their subjects' legal demands; that Austria (through his Hungarian intervention) was at his obéisance, while France was internally neutralised, and England, Alas! made use of for his purposes. And then he dictated the *Warsaw-protocol,* proposing a successor who may have become ingratiated to the Danes by being the only Schleswigholstein prince who took up arms against his country. Therefore did I call Czar Nicholas father of the London Treaty, which was his final achievement. Our Cabinet has been blind enough to assist in a Revival of already abandoned succession-rights. Only **two** lives protect us at this moment from the chance of Russia claiming inheritauce in Schleswig-Holstein as well as in Denmark! We had to cross more distant devices by very bloody sacrifices in the Crimea—and here certain parties are exciting us into a war against our vital interests!? — — —

I give in a Supplement extracts from a "Memorial" which the late well-known Prussian Ambassador Chevalier Bunsen delivered to Lord Palmerston, July 1850, which may be called prophetic.

And I dismiss said Protocol by quoting a striking Reservation which the noble S.-Holst. prince of Noer makes in a Protest against the over-riding of his rights (London, 24th March, 1853), viz.:—

> "The treaty of the 8th May, against which I have lodged
> this day my protest with the English Government, I hold to
> be one of coercion and spoliation; nevertheless there is one

---

given over, for example: 645 cannon with proportionate masses of ammunition, 413,000 uniforms, 16 various war-craft, and even quantities of raw material and utensils. The *direct* sacrifice alone made by Schleswig-Holstein amounts to 19,400,000 Prussian dollars!

condition, to obtain which I would make every sacrifice—it is that an arrangement shall be come to similar to that which was made in respect to the crowns of Spain and France at the treaty of Utrecht; so that the crowns of Denmark and Russia shall never be united on the same head, and Denmark and the Duchies be thereby incorporated with the Russian Empire."

Thus the sinful Seeds were sown for untold slow sufferings, for the present bloodshed and danger. Shall we persist in the same Errors, and thereby render ourselves guilty of making all Europe miserable?—

Even in 52—although by Such injustice—another, *a last chance* was given into the hands of Denmark (similar to that final appeal of Franklin). For then the disappointment and desperate wrath against the executioners was, if possible, even greater than against the enemy. It was such that, on his foresaking Schleswig-Holstein in 60, the present Commander-in-chief, Fieldmarshal Wrangel, had to fly for his life, and that even the innocent Prussian troops were insulted and attacked. The leading men, the best soldiers, &c., expatriated themselves. Even then the Schleswig-Holsteiners might have been lulled into resignation and hum-drum contentment with such an, anyways not enviable, rôle, viz. of being cut off from their great nation, in order to pamper the ambition of an X class kingdom. Common sense and fairness *might* have accomplished much if Denmark had adopted the only possible course of a faithful approach, and leaning on the conciliatory nation to which Schleswig-Holstein belongs and which might have become her truest friend. The long-suffering of Germans is so great; take for example the case of conquered Alsace, where the French respected nationality and reap the fruits. (It is true they have a different political position to offer into the bargain!)

How did the Danes employ the last 13 *years of Respite?*—Why, by doing everything in their power to deserve enmity and con-tempt. They broke down the last pillars of the Schleswig-Holstein Charter, and the crash ensued.—After the Schleswig-Holsteiners had been delivered over, bound, new aggressions ensued—indeed sur-passing everything previous. But I shall rewrite and modify some expressions, because since this article was begun (2nd Feb.) a most just Retribution has swept away the Invaders with avalanche-like rapidity. Nor can it be my intention to charge the Danes generally with those wrongs, which have been carried out with bold bravery worthy of a better cause. I would rather omit entirely the following if the statement was not unavoidable as a voucher for the very *very* strong doses which S.-H. endured until her habitual phlegma was aroused, and secondly for the inevitable judgment which Denmark has brought upon herself.—

Up to that "Copenhagen insurrection" a Statthalter (Vice-regent) had governed the Duchies, from Schleswig-city, in connection with the "Schlesw.-Holst. Kanzlei" (Office) in Copenhagen. Since 52 the administration was split in-two, and consequently the power of self-protection still more reduced. As to Self-government?—a finished machinery of foreign and of servile renegade-Officials was set up, whose tacitly understood leading qualification and duty was the *Danification* of S.-H. It may easily be supposed that but few men possessing self-respect could be found for such errands. With most unabating perseverance the strongest temptations were held out for abdication of national honour, while those who remained true were hunted down in many extraordinary ways to despair and poverty. (In a Supplement I give extracts from a document which describes the fate of the town of Hadersleben, drawn up by the citizens; you'll find it to speak a strange history.)—I will here only state how out of 900 higher officials there were about 800 Danes. Almost every imaginable office and many civic appointments likewise (physicians, apothecaries, &c.) were thus beset— even *the Church* was desecrated to become a lever of Danish propoganda. And what a class of men they were, who accepted such bread-offices—under the crushing hatred of the population—and, it must be acknowledged, disrespected even by honourable Danes, particularly of the army. Mean, crafty, spying, incessantly worrying, withholding justice; the greater number of inadequate abilities and a many of low morals—they, in fact, more resembled Chinese Mandarines. Danish soldiers invaded the country, and backed up the system, while the home-troops (likewise those specially belonging to the German Confederation) were marched abroad. The best

2

citizens were driven away, the press fettered, the right of public
meetings, &c., denied, votes pressed by threats and stratagem,
facts falsified even officially,* the voice of the people gagged to
such an extent that heavy fines were levied even upon written
petitions. To make the measure run over, even the domestic
rights were violated: men were forbidden to have German house-
teachers, even as friends; persons were searched for the special
S.-H. (German) money, which is one of the prerogatives of the
country. The persecutions were extended beyond the grave. Witness Flensburg, for there the memorials of German warriors were
effaced, and their sites (as well as those of about 100 private
graves) were abused, as the footing of a "Lion-monument" intend-
ing to represent a scornful emblem of supposed victory and defiance
against Germany.—The attacks on nationality were more serious
than a "Dictionary-quarrel" (Times): About 100,000 of the most
pious Christians expelled from their churches; a still greater number of children seriously injured in their education, and thus their
prospects in life thwarted by being forcibly danified- while every
Dane, in order to get on, must learn German, or English, or
French.—Also the pecuniary interests of Schleswigholstein were
deeply injured. Not so mnch by the large sums which left the
country for Copenhagen; even more so by hurting the very roots of
the country's material welfare, which decidedly preponderate south-
ward in Germany, where the chief vent for their produce and
cattle, as well as their best markets for purchasing are situated;
where they get money and credit; where they find employment
for their shipping, sailors, men, &c In fact, this interest of trade,
caused by natural position and advantages, radiates strongly from
northern Germany, particularly Hamburg, even to Jutland and all
Scandinavia.—Altogether the sway of Denmark bore the brand of
petty, selfish tyranny, insulting arrogance, falsehold; and deeply

* In 61 the Diet of Holstein marvelled to learn—through our House of Lords—
an official Danish announcement "that the said Government had consented to lay
the whole Budget before them for their deliberate vote thereon." On their inter-
pellation however, the Minister and Commissary Raaslöff was honourable enough
to avow:—"I could but have answered with an *unconditional No;* consequently un-
conditionally denying that there had been or could be any question of laying a
budget (before the Diet) for resolution-." (Quotation from "The policy and
'Misunderstandings' of the Danish Government." Pages 43 and 52.)

injurious to the morals, because it set a premium on servility, attempted to root out manly national independence, torturing and grinding down body and soul. It had not the strength to carry out fusillades, transportations, &c.' (which, however, arouse man's energetic redress); but it resembled the incessant assaults of musquitoes, whom you cannot evade, and you sink at last an ignominous prey. It has even been admitted on the Danish side, the destruction of the present generation did not matter so long as the country was gained, particularly Scheswig.*—And such destruction of prosperity has been but too far carried into effect at the sacrifice of those preeminently patriotic South-Schleswigers.—The value of their estates has been depreciated very considerably; and to indicate how they were eaten up by the Danish army, before the war commenced, I give only one example of an acquaintance of my own: an Estate-owner who possed 400 cattle is reduced to one-half, and forced to fetch—from yon rich export-country!—pork, &c., out of Hamburg. Yet such a lot is enviable in comparison to that of those unhappy Schleswigholsteiners, who are still forced in the Danish army to fight against their own countrymen.

Such a case of systematic, wearing-out oppression has perhaps never been equalled.—

Suddenly the 15th Nov., 1863 cut through and did away all those violated and incomplete diplomatic patchwork-attempts, and then the case all at once recovered its inherent clearness. Can you be astonished that the inhabitants see the hand of God in this, and they as well as every honourable German declared, they would not be sold any longer?—

Schleswigholstein has **come of age,** and demands possession of the *patrimonial Estate* from the former Guardian, who has enjoyed all its benefits rent-free for so long a period. Was it kind of the latter to attempt willing away his Ward's Trust-property,

* "In short, a mode of Government was established, which English Ambassadors and Consular-agents abroad have justly stigmatised as a '*system of terrorism,*' and *intimidation*—as an *unbearable tyranny* 'quite at *variance with the spirit of the age*'—as an odious oppression calculated to render the country 'the scene of agitation, perhaps of tumult and revolt.'" (See *Blue Book,* Correspond. respecting the affairs of S. and H., 1860–61. Dispatch of Mr. Cons.-gen. Ward to Lord J. Russell, p. 29; do. of Mr. Howard to the same, p. 91; *Lord J. Russell's* (!) to Mr. Howard, p. 99.) [Quotation from "A plain Statement of the S.-H. question."]

under the pretence of a superannuation of benefits, a lapse-lease?
What say the Witnesses of that extraordinary Will? (the London
Treaty).—

After the death of the late King-Duke, when the German nation
and Diet were preparing to carry out the long overdue Execution,
what did the Danes do? Why, the first act of their new King
was, to strike Germany in the face by sanctioning the long prepared Incorporation of Schleswig. Now this was a rupture of the
Peace-treaty with Germany, as well as of the special condition
under which Austria and Prussia had acceded to the London
Treaty. If the latter had even possessed binding validity before,
that act of Denmark would have upset it. Still nearly a quarter
of a year further grace was allowed, until the German Powers lost
patience and appealed to the "ultimo ratio."

At this point England attempted to draw that *German* affair
before *a European Congress,* or rather a sort of tribunal to carry
out our Ministers' favourite Treaty—the same England having a
few weeks previously put down the very idea of such a Congress.
But it seems to me that Germany might with equal right have
asked England to submit the claims of those "rebellious" Indian
Princes to a similar forum.—It was even reported that France and
the other powers have been entreated to join in a general enforcing-
League against Germany! and certainly a number of threats and
War-cries were trumpeted abroad by England.—

A rank blasphemy was thrown at Austria and Prussia for declining to *suspend hostilities another 6 weeks!?* "to give the Danish
Rigsraad time to reassemble," whilst this body had been adjourned
only a day or two previously, after finally resolving upon a most
decided *persistence* in their deliberate *assault!* A glaring comment
to this: From the German Peace of 51 until 59, say 8 *years,* were
given to Denmark to carry out her engagements (although arbitrarily reduced to a measure quite inadequate to the rights of
Schleswigholstein). Answer: new encroachments, as indicated.
At last the Diet threatened military execution of its domains.
Answer: evasions for the term of five—yes 5 *years* (because it took
them so long to strengthen their "Dannewerk"). Then took place
the last Danish Duke's death, and further as above. Another 6

weeks' suspense? Their cards are now open, and show that, besides the evident calculation, thereby to evade the frost-impediment of their fortifications and of their fleet (and to get the use of the English fleet too, if possible!), they required that time for finally completing and manning their immense works. A Danish paper advised a suspension of the incorporation, it is true; disclosing, however, with a peculiar candour, that a fitter opportunity must be awaited for attaining their ends—how can any foreign power give a guarantee, * where treaties and engagements have been violated for 13 years, when Earl Russell himself admitted already in 61:—"It is unfortunately a notorious fact that none of the guarantees given to Germany (by Denmark) have been respected."—

On what grounds has England rejoiced in the *liberation of Italy*, taking an active part in it, and making no objections to the armed interference of France? You may well grant Italy her due; you may well give a free people's reception to her noble Hero – but how can it be excused that you withhold the same acknowledgment from S.-Holstein and Germany! If that admirable Garibaldi (whom I would be delighted to shake by the hand) knew the merits of this case: be assured he would embrace it with all his heart, because he would discover that S.-Holstein may be most aptly called *the Lombardy of Denmark!* And, to do justice, let it never be forgotten that Austria did not misgovern in that degree as Denmark, that, on the contrary, she conferred many material advantages on Lombardy, and that her title of possession was fully *legitimate.—*

The Liberation of S.-Holstein had been but too long delayed. Every coming day increased the sufferings of the abandoned Schleswigers, from whom empoverishing war-requisitions were levied; every day made the situation more perilous for the whole country. The German nation demanded justice; and Austria has officially notified that a denial of this demand would have caused civil war. Indeed, where is there a case to equal the sacrifices made, and the patient long suffering (bordering on disgrace) which Germany has endured for 13 years?! This tenacious and unostenta-

---

* And *most* strange: our Ministers have lately explained, that it is a mistake—that a guarantee never has been offered!

tious bravery, though less captivating than Italian impetuosity, is certainly more considerate toward others. Notwithstanding Lord Ellenborough, if there ever was a *righteous* war, that which defends the rights of the Schleswigholsteiners assuredly is.

It was the overwhelming influence of a case so uniquely clear and just, which performed the miracle of putting an end to long-inrooted divisions, and of bringing the just and chivalrously-noble aspirations of the German nation to Unity. *The Germans feel the liberation of their kindred country, imposed upon them as* **a religious duty.** The expelled victims of Danish oppression, who had found refuge in the interior, became the apostles for the liberation of S.-H. There is much similarity between this movement and the reformation of Luther; only that in this case the nation is turned as one man against assault from abroad. And at the same time the Germans begin to see how long they have been blind to that destructive Danish Wedge which was driven right into Northern-Germany. How is it possible that England could overlook the importance of that great national vote given at Frankfurt, by parliamentary delegates from all parts and all partie of the German People—some 500—all, without one dissent for the protection of Schleswigholstein?!—*Vox populi, vox Dei.*—

Extraordinary developement: Austria and Prussia—against their own will and against that of the nation—have become the instruments of repurchasing with their own blood that liberty which they once sacrificed to the enemy!* This is the first instalment; and it would be unjust to the chivalrous dispositions of the Emperor and the Father-in-law of our Princess Victoria, to doubt but what, true to the honour of their nationality, they could forsake their championship only half completed. Prussia in particular is in honour bound to fulfil the engagements specially entered into The Germans will fulfil their duty. Does any thinking man fancy that a nation of 45 millions can be scare-crowed? Learn from history that, however peace-loving and over-indulgent, *fear* does *not* influence this nation, which has vanquished the most powerful adversaries, the ancient Romans as well as the armies of the

---

* And those same S.-Holstein arms and guns are now used against them, that they delivered into the hands of the enemy in 52!

greatest conquerer of our century. (I speak as an eye-witness of that unparalleled patriotic rising of 1814.) Should Germany ask for friends; why, Switzerland, America, Russia are all more or less now convinced of the justice of the Schleswigholstein cause. And it deserves particular acknowledgment that even France, where a certain jealousy might have been more explainable, has (already given numerous proofs of coming to a fair and chivalrous acknow-ledgment.—And England — —

I wish I could convey some faint idea of that glorious day of Liberation * which dawned upon Schleswigholstein through so threatening a winter's sky. You cannot appreciate it without knowing the cool sobriety of their political character (resembling our Yorkshiremen or the Dutch), their immense sacrifices in the late war, their full knowledge of the renewed and even greater responsibility, risks and dangers, hanging over head like heavy thunderstorms. In every town, village, district, as soon as the usurping power were removed, by an innate impulse the inhabitants assembled, all heads were uncovered, all hearts lifted up, bursting forth in religious Anthems:—

> "Now give all thanks to God,
>   With hands and hearts and voices;
> Who mighty deeds hath done
>   This day. Our soul rejoices!"

Or Luther's warrior-song, which led the young protestants to victory:—

> "A stronghold castle is our God,
> A trusty shield and weapon."

The next thing was, to swear allegiance to the new Duke; to remove *unscathed* some of those most cruel tools of foreign oppres-

---

* And yet there is a dark shade to this bright picture, which a German would desire to veil. But it appears to me that exactly thereby the urgency of a total reform is proved still more impressively. That blow of being forsaken by Germany, with all the consequences of oppression, has fallen upon S.-H. with too overwhelming a force; a part of the weaker-minded have fallen into despairing apathy, that worst of all enemies, and this disease is not removed by the continuing uncertainty about the intentions of Austria and Prussia. Otherwise you would see more active demonstrations, and less of that it would appear to me excessive long-suffering. But now—beside such men as Hansen of Flensburg, Capts. Decker and Lassen of Sylt, Lieut. Rathlev of Kiel—you meet with a number of renegades (like that Blauenfeldt) who have fallen into deplorable extremes.

sion;* to secure order and well-being. On all sides you would
hear the national air "Schleswigholstein sea-surrounded" to the
thrilling strains of which they have so often fought victoriously,
and which has long become a national song all over Germany,
similar to the "Marseillaise." Volunteers pressed forward by
thousands, mourning that they were so long prevented proving
their devotion unto death. Monster deputations were sent to the
Duke, several under great risk from parts which swarmed with
the enemy; and what a dignified language they spoke! I must
particularly observe that the Duke's family was unpopular; more
than for his legitimate right he was chosen as *their deliverer from
Denmark.* There are not to be found anywhere more fervent Germans than in the *border* Duchy of Schleswig. Ladies will hear
with pleasure what a noble part the fair sex of S.-H. took and
maintains in patriotic actions—for they resigned all pleasures
which brought them into contact with Danes; they had their sons
instructed in the use of arms; they were and are at home with
the wounded and sick.—Business and preparations for the future
are now resumed without ostentation, but with an altered bearing;
a weight is removed from the brow; an air of inward contentment
meets you; everything goes on in the most orderly manner now,
as it were by itself. The German soldiers, who liberated their
countrymen—not hirelings, but *citizens* of all classes—could not
avoid deep emotion, admiration and fraternising with the grateful
Schleswigholsteiners; and they have proved by their deeds, their
exemplary conduct and endurance, that they know what they are
fighting for.—Some of your Newspaper-correspondents are beginning to catch a glimpse of these things.—

Every Conservative has particular reason to rejoice that this
"chronic disease" has been cured by strictly *legal* means; **Schleswigholstein being now for ever cut off from Den-
mark,** exactly as England from Hannover through the accession
of our Queen Victoria. But, in case this were all different, in the

* Let it be distinctly stated—for misrepresentations are to be anticipated—that
the German Commissaries protected these Danish officials much more than impartially,
first awaiting proofs for offences or incapacity; even to the damage of their own
Army; for most of those that were spared continue acting as secret spies, several
have been apprehended.

face of any existing treaties, or new paper-chains yet to be invented: Schleswigholstein is **doubly lost** to Denmark by the law of God, by the dictate of humanity, by the voice of the people, all which entail irrevocable punishment upon breach of trust and tyranny. Not one of the dozen or so cases, where the "eternal" treaties of Vienna were broken, possesses such an undeniable claim to the sympathy of every fairthinking man.

And England?—Indeed, the English Ministry was the only party to break a considerate silence—they have demanded the putting-down of such "demonstrations" as a "breach of good-faith" (!). * But you, *the People of England,* have not *you* a word for Schleswig-holstein, for the honour of our free country?—

Errors respecting S.-Holstein corrected : †

Why, they are incessantly springing up like Fungusses from a neglected field! to be expelled only by a thorough sub-soil drainage —by the simple remedy of *truth.* Such poisonous food has already caused an aversion against plain fare—any story is devoured with eagerness that puts down the German cause; whether it be the killing of so many German soldiers, or the death of a King of Bavaria. It is perfectly clear to an impartial eye, that any proofs for the righteous cause are put aside wherever possible.—

I have already torn out several fundamental Errors, touching the *London Treaty, Integrity of Denmark, Balance of power,* as well as that shortsighted Scheme for a *Cutting-up of S.-Holstein,* and the *Pretence of any Guarantee* on the part of England, of 1720 or any other year. I will continue to explain various other Errors and Accusations—although that trouble might be spared in case people once took pains to *learn the facts.* For example:—

"The triviality of the object in question, to excite a general war, has been charged against Germany. Now—unless my memory fails me—we have more than once fought or offered fight

---

* *One very smart correction* they have met with from the Saxon Minister M. von Beust.

† A Danish official statement has appeared, respecting the present state of Schleswig. Now I would recommend its correctness to be cross-examined by what the party immediately concerned has to say (of which a specimen in my Supplement). Altogether, if our press was to devote only 50 per cent. of their diligence to investigate the actions of the accused side, the balance would result decidedly in favour of Germany.

to protect one or two of our countrymen ("Trent"-affair), and I am proud of this. Now Schleswigholstein contains 900,000 inhabitants, and I do not know why they should not be worth protecting, as much as an equal number of Englishmen.—

As to **Germany exciting a general war,** I better leave the answer to the French paper *Monde* (of 5th Jan.):—"The .violations of right on the side of Denmark have given new confirma-"tion to the righteous cause of Germany, and G. does no longer "feel disposed to let this unexpected advantage escape once more. "The case in question is of narrow compass; it can in no wise "lead to a European conflict, unless the Great-powers seize hold "of it as *a pretext* to fight one onother."—

Other **false Origins** for the troubles of Schleswigholstein are pleaded by her enemies, or those who ignore the real source, viz.:—

1) *The senior Duke of S.-H.-Augustenburg,* the scape-goat of the Eider-Danes. Now 20 years back his rights were not only acknowledged, but (as I am further assured by creditable men) overtures made to him by his Brother-in-law, the King of Denmark, for the inheritance of that crown likewise (I have been told by Danish soldiers that even in the Army this was expected);—the Duke, however, refused, and the Danish policy was then altered, as described. This point deserves research. Anyhow, the fact is clear by the "Open Letter Patent," that the legitimate succession-rights of the Duke have been arbitrarily attacked six years previous to the London Treaty. Of course, he protested against a violation of his eventual claims on S.-Holstein, and gained the acknowledgment of Prussia; but as to the defensive steps taken by the S.-H. parliament, it is proved that he was on his estate and informed unawares of their resolutions. Nor would he have been the man; for on account of high-toryism he was quite unpopular. The error as to his having sold a resignation I have already exposed.

2) *The Lawyers and Professors* are called the originators (and the Danes have done all they could to eradicate their presence). One might as well say that Clergymen *create* religion; for both are only the organs of their respective duties. And that the men of law and learning have the particular duty of protecting the laws and historical rights of their country will not be. contended.

3) *The Nobility of S.-H.* are accused. Now this corporation reminds us of a glorious fact that adorns our history; for with us
likewise the rights of the people have been fought for by the
noblemen; but those of S.-II. have certainly as little as ours over-
stepped the duties they owed to the Sovereign. If you will refer
to our Copenhagen Ambassador's report of 26th Nov. last, you will
find some strong confirmation from the mouth of Baron v. Scheel-
Plessen. And as an indication of the determination which is alive
in S.-II., I will add, that this same deserving man, although he
was for a number of years highly honoured as their leader in the
Holstein Diet, has now lost the people's confidence by declining
a decided acknowledgment of the new Duke.

Then again are brought forward as "Invaders." 4) *the German
Governments* (Lord Cowley!) and *particularly Prussia.* This sounds
like a rebuke on the degree to which these parties have neglected
the protection of their nation's interest. The first condition for
vanquishing Denmark would have been a Fleet. Now a country,
possessing the second greatest commercial-shipping in Europe (far
exceeding France), and supplying some 10 or 20,000 mariners to
other nations, might or rather *ought* to have a Navy to protect it
against the Danes anyhow!?—But the scarcely believable facts are:
that at the commencement of the previous war Germany was without one ship of war; that in 51 the beginnings of a fleet were
put to the hammer, and that—after 16 years' time—Denmark can
still *think* of blockading all the ports of Germany!!—You'll laugh
at this—and so did I, until I understood the unfortunate reasons.

The preceding at the same time elucidates, why *the military
position of Denmark* is considerally more favourable than super-
ficially supposed. The present fights prove what a large army of
the best soldiers [can be held at bay by sea-side fortifications,
seconded by a fleet which can throw landing-forces here or there
at pleasure. 'T is the fight between Lion and Sea-horse, either
intact in his domain. (It is not necessary to name those other
strong Allies of Denmark, the disunity of Germany and foreign
Interference.) —

One of our papers fears that the *Danish elements* in North-
Schleswig may be *hurt* by the separation. But as little as such a

thing was heard of until a perfect concord was interrupted by an opposition artificially engendered: so is the spirit of equity already reintroduced, and they will soon see that instead of losing they will gain. There have already been cases where those *Danish* peasants have petitioned the new government for school instruction of the *German* language, &c.

Among the latest untruths I find the reported *rebellion* of a number of *Italian* or *Hungarian* troops in Jutland. If you want to know the reality: these troops take an interest in the liberation of S.-H.! because they begin to understand the analogy.

Then again under a hundred garbs that **Pity** *for Denmark* is revived, lately by an "official" representation. How is it possible that such moves can have any weight since our own Blue-book accounts (although partly long suppressed) prove that the so-called Martyrs are only thwarted in an unfair speculation, to gain S.-H. or at least Schleswig, no matter how—and certainly against law, liberty, and humanity.--Unfortunately not a tithe of the sufferings of S.-Holstein is known to England.

I have seen threatning allusions in our papers, as to France adopting the precedent by *seizing the German Rhinelands*. But the French nation will be more wise than take such bad advice, not forgetting that the very contrary case exists, the German province of Alsace being a pawn of peace in their hands.—And as to . threatening Austria with Hungary, there was little tact in that — let us not forget Ireland.

Another attack on the Germans I have observed with regret. It is the taunt to reform first their own *internal evils*. No nation is more candid (I must call it excessively so) in laying these bare; and *we* have no idea of the troubles and difficulties connected with their reform. But everybody knows that man and wife, though quarrelling, unite when the house is attacked from without.—

The greatest Error, however, that you possibly could fall into would be, to imagine "that the Germans be already wavering and flagging." Their devotion for a righteous cause is extraordinary. Baron v. Stein (perhaps the greatest statesman of the past age, and who preeminently organised the resusciation of Russia and Germany 50 years ago) said from his experience, "that of all nations of the time present, *the Germans probably are best capacitated for a regular and tenacious Movement.*"—There is a lull caused by the acknowledgment due to the German Powers for their first steps of a cure. But let changing aspects require it, and you will see a proportionate resistance developed. Or even, in case it should be deemed unavoidable to submit for the moment: you may take your oath that the very next opportunity would renew the effort which cannot fail ultimately to succeed. *The Crisis is overcome:* **the Germans will never give up half-way!**—

Have we not in our own history the most striking example of what such struggles against nationality lead to? That Norman King who conquered our country left us a glorious but bloody Legacy—but after the struggles of ages and ages, what remains of the same but the Channel-islands and a yet lingering division? —although happily mitigated.—

What shall I say to the greedily devoured Tales of plunder, illtreatment, the *barbarisms* against Denmark, &c., which go the round? worse than that ill-renowned Tartar's fables from Sewastopel. The *Times* correspondent (21st) boasts of his wish "that may sound somewhat savage and inhuman from a neutral (?), viz., that the German soldiers might dash their heads against the ramparts of Fridericia" (although he is very genteelly rebuked by his adversary colleague [24th inst.]). Now the reverend son of our great Wilberforce has lately made a most serious charge (respecting false statements of the St. Jago Catastrophe); all I have to say is, that *in the S.-Holstein case our press has a brilliant chance to clear itself!*—

One thing I had almost omitted, the striking circumstance that some High-Tories of Germany (*Kreuzzeitung's*-party) likewise attack the cause, and they from their side accuse it of an origin exactly contrary to others, viz., the democratic elements of Germany!

Is it not a relief, then, to fly from all such diplomatic and other meddles and muddles, and to see only to the simple reality? which lays unfurled before all who will not close their eyes.

"Deliverance from Denmark" is the overwhelmingly anxious watchword of all men of character in Schleswigholstein.—For the guidance of those who like to go by figures, I will here communicate that the Danes, in only 13 years (after payment of the

cost of administration), are estimated to have drawn out of this small country the Net amount of 50 Millions of Thalers — say 7 Mill. £'s.! But for any man of higher points of view, the moral and mental Sufferings and Injuries, which have resulted from so unnatural a tie, will be decisive. To single out one example: if only the amount of sufferings were weighed, endured by those S.-H. soldiers whose sole crime was that they refused to fight their countrymen and liberators! Particularly the Schleswigers, the hardships and risks under which a many of them have escaped are extraordinary — and a number are still enduring such misery.—

After having thus drawn up the Items of the long account between Germany and Denmark, and proceeding to strike the *final Balance:* the conclusion results, that the Credits preponderate on the side of the S.-Holsteiners and Germans in a surprising degree. *A revolutionary* **Coup d'état** *has been perpetrated on them through foreign Interference and pressure, which not only violated the Charter of S.-H., but attempted the formation of a League* (London Treaty) *for upsetting the lawful heir to its throne, thus directly attacking the Integrity of Germany.*

The assault on Schleswigholstein is a deep laid *diplomatic* and *party Movement.* It injures the People's Constitutional Rights generally of all nations, since *it attempts to shake that essentially conservative principle* of an equitable division of power between the People and the rulers. The unfortunate Danish people are strengthend in their passions, and hurried into extremes to the brink of self-destruction! And the passions of our own people have been worked up likewise — *we* are to become *the final tool* for wrongs which go against our honour and vital interests! —

Should not every one of us then not only put a stop to such abuse, but, on the contrary, actively come to the rescue of that which is our happiness and glory, that well regulated Freedom embracing *all* the members of society? —

Here are further proofs for the unfortunate *Interference of England:* —

Germany had in the very beginning of the dispute in all confidence and faith accepted the mediation of England. An Englishman was then admitted as an umpire between the German and Danish governors of Schleswig, but did not make good that name England became the main Instrument of an unjust Peace and of that ominous London Treaty – whereas it lay in our hands to have brought the whole affair to an end *then.* – But still England's chance continued for years. Our first meagre acknowledgments of the S.-H. cause by Sir H. Verney, how gratefully were they received! And I need only draw attention to the fate of E. Russell's new plan for a Settlement (1862, Sept. 24), which the Germ. Governments so readily accepted, although it involved a considerable sacrifice of rights on their part. Now our Government have frequently acknowledged that great wrongs have been committed by the Danes, and several of their leading Members have made the almost unparalleled avowal "that *they did not understand the S.-H. case themselves*" (!) – how then could they dare to undertake an Interference and to such a degree that good luck alone has saved our involving all Europe into the horrors of a general War!

Such a "Policy" against S.-Holstein and Germany is utterly inexplicable, except by imaginary Interests of England. These are generally not spoken, only hinted at in vague allusions, such as the balance of power. But let us not shrink from examining the value of such lurking calculations. – Is it imagined that through Denmark we can protect the Baltic? Why, the facts of history entirely contradict this, for D. could not uphold its neutrality even when she possessed Norway to boot. – And as to Germany, it is proved by a marked one-sidedness, that a certain jealousy exists against her regaining what belongs to her. This may perhaps call forth contradictions – but I ask for *facts* to disprove it. And I further assert, that only short-sightedness on our part can give some explanation for *the absence* of a lively interest, which ought to exist in our country for everyting that tends to restore Germany to Unity and strength. I intend to give reasons further on, why I consider such a developement of Germany the one thing *most desirable for our interests.*

Meanwhile I must repeat the opinion, that almost the entire blame of the present war rests upon ourselves, so long as we do not correct the proceedings on the part of our Government.

But the tide of justice has taken a decided turn—no King Canute can command it to recede, altho' the struggle may be either short or protracted. Although once foiled in a War of the most gallant nature (so that S.-Holstein has been termed the Switzerland of the North) and the victim of a tyrannical scheme: yet "The Rights of a Nation do never supperannuate." * And the time is sure to come when the very name of Schleswigholstein will mark a Case of unimpeachable justice, long and cruelly abused, but through perseverance gallantly triumphant in the end.

Messrs. Bazley, M. P., and Potter have (at that praiseworthy Manchester meeting of 12th Febr.) just in time exposed the fact that "the London Treaty, the result of secret Diplomacy, has never been presented to our Parliament." And what is much more—it has since become evident, that our Ministry is not willing to give the Representatives of S.-H. a chance of deciding their own destiny! Recollect that they are the only party that *elected* a King of Denmark as their Duke under conditions which have now expired, and that consequently they are the very tribunal of decision, subject only to the approval of Germany.

Indeed it is the highest time for our people's Representatives to prove to the world that in England "there is behind the Ministry and behind the Throne a grand Court of Appeal in the last resort. Till they know the opinion of this potent body, they do not really know the opinions by which our policy will be guided."

It is the noblest Perogative, as well as Responsibllity of our Parliament, to protect from infringment the just cause of the people, at home and abroad. Englishmen, stand forward, and do an act of signal Justification before the world. Throw into the scales your moral weight, "not for a temporary and patched-up

---

* *Prof. Waitz, the weighty authority of Göttingen, thus concludes his legal opinion on the Claims of Duke Frederick VIII.:—*

"The right (title) of the Sovereign and the right and will of the People have never been found in better harmony than in this case.

Everything that upholds the order of States is founded upon a union between these two conditions.

In case one of them be injured, then order is disturbed. If both be disregarded, then it is upset entirely.

That such should not take place, is demanded by the interests of all People and all Sovereigns."

peace, but *a permanent peace,*" such as will insure the just rights
and thus the Well-being of all parties.—Estrangement exists, errors
have been committed: but to acknowledge and set these right—
and that with a noble good grace—is a Triumph which deserves
the greatest acknowledgment, and which is followed by the blessings
of the All-Just.—

This is the most urgent question now at issue before the Grand-
Jury of our Nation: *Shall we allow* **England to be made
the tool for enslaving Schleswigholstein?**—and our
Country probably will have to give **a casting Vote.**

II.

SUGGESTIONS FOR A RADICAL CURE!

"Brilliant hopes are beckoning us forward, almost dazzling after
the miseries we have gone through. We are, however, well aware
that our final aim is not yet achieved. Your Highness does not yet
govern your own country, and not we ourselves have chased away
the Danes. The supreme Lords of those gallant soldiers who have
sacrificed their blood have not yet declared their intention to restore
S -Holstein to none other but to itself and its legitimate Sovereign.
We are well aware that to fully realise our rights every one of us
must strain all his powers, and we are ready to *stake* everything in
order to *gain* Everything. We long for the moment, when we shall
be able to defend our country against the Danes, under the leader-
ship of your Highness, through our own strength. We rely upon
the righteousness of our cause; we believe in the assistance of the
Almighty; we are inspired by the indomitable Confidence that:
Success must finally be ours! Now or never! *Free from Denmark,*
that is our watchword!" *

SHALL *such* an Appeal be heard unheeded?—Who dares to impose
upon his country for a second time the responsibility of enforcing
a patched-up peace, with all its unavoidable injuries and dangers,
for the tranquility and Well-being not only of Schleswigholstein,
but of Europe?!

* Extract from the Homage-address delivered by the *Schleswig* Monster-deputation, numbering 15 to 1600 *chosen Representatives* of the *whole* Duchy, to Duke
Frederick VIII, at Kiel, on the 26th Feb., 1864. It deserves notice at same time,
that this Sovereign—notwithstanding an unfavourable prestige, and notwithstanding
that Austria and Prussia, instead of any favouritism, attempted to expel him from
the country—has nevertheless already gained by his private character a warm
popularity. The only thing that a great portion of the Schleswigholsteiners blame
him for, is, that he did not boldly place himself at their head from the beginning,
defying any resistance.

The man who would think about upsetting once more the *fait accompli* of this Liberation, would advocate something that is worse than a second Poland;—he had far better recommend Austria to conquer back Lombardy, for A. has at least a legal title.

What difficulties are there in the way against according justice to S.-Holstein and Germany?

As soon as we gain an exalted comprehensive point of view to survey the position of Europe, the discovery will be made that most of the present difficulties and dangers are actually created by ourselves!

The inward tendency of European affairs is indeed generally favourable—the task is not to distort them by unwise interference. The restoration of Unity in *Italy,* how promising; and, in case it be followed out by peaceable means, it is to be hoped not ultimately opposed by Austria. As to unfortunate *Poland,* as things have come to pass, would not her best friends perhaps do well to limit their endeavours to the gain of a similarly independent position as that enjoyed by Norway? for at last the Poles and Russians are only branches of the same race. Respecting *Hungary* I am of opinion that a similar arrangement, together with the regenerating Austria, would be the most favourable solution; and the great number of Germans in Hungary form a natural link of intimate alliance. Blot out Austria from the map of Europe, and what is to become of those smaller nationalities? which it is by no means an easy task to hold together. On the contrary, I believe that those unsettled *Danubian principalities* would be better off if connected with the "Empire of the Danube" (and it has been very appropriately argued that they would form a set off against Lombardo-Venetia).

The most important contest of the present time is that respecting *S.-Holstein,* because it is *the very left arm of Germany,* that has been so long maimed, and the amputation of which was attempted through the Treaty of London. What then hinders a natural and just solution?

The spell by which the course of natural events was once mournfully reversed, exists no more. The present Emperor of **Russia** seeks to increase his Empire by *inward* reforms and developement

—as far away as on the banks of the Amur we see his colonies springing up.

And as to **France,** her Emperor Napoleon has long ago pronounced that London Treaty *"an impotent document."* Indeed, the course of France deserves acknowledgment more and more, and she seems actually to take the lead in proposing a general Vote that shall be asked (same as in Mexico) from the people in S.-Holstein.

England, England again and now almost alone, interferes in a manner that baffles comprehension.

Now the appearance of some new light stirs up our country even in the case of a condemned criminal. And here you were on the point of committing fraternicide—after only a half and one-sided hearing! Seeing you in the act of pronouncing an unjust Verdict against our only brother-nation—whose language you no more understand—I claim it as my right and duty to stand forth as an Interpreter, demanding you to beware and reconsider coolly the simple Facts.

The part which our country took against a small overpowered and neglected German State has long and increasingly troubled my mind. Latterly my sentiments have approached toward disgust—what then shall the Germans think of us!—But I now feel comforted by this belief, that a simple *practical* explanation will set the matter right pretty soon (of which description I suppose that "Letter from S.-H." to be, in Bradshaw's March number).

It strikes me, the Enigma so incomprehensable to you must have been this, *that parts of Germany should ever have been allowed to get into such an ambiguous connection with a* **foreign** *country!* And, truly as no one can serve two masters: it was the highest time to cure radically such duplicity.—So far you never mastered the subject, but gave it up long ago as "interminable and incomprehensible." Hearsay and its variations in leading-articles took the place of facts. And now an inrooted prejudice of a many years' growth keeps your better judgment captive. *

---

* It must be the very enormity of the case which rendered it so strangely unintelligible to you. You did not understand how a large Country could possibly allow one of its Members to have been so long ill-treated by the gross arrogance

Let me pave the way by being the first to make the avowal
how long I myself have been guilty of that unfortunate bias into
which our well-grounded national honour is so liable to degenerate,
bringing injuries upon others and ourselves. At last most of the
facts, which I now communicate, *forced* themselves upon me by
their undeniable reality.—And in these days I have seen such tough
and unflinching Englishmen likewise converted, that I begin to
believe in miracles!

There can be no doubt about it: *Our country has committed
serious wrongs against Germany,*—aggravated by *absence of common
courtesy* and by poignant *sneers directed against misfortunes.* And
towards Denmark we have been only a bad friend.—An instinctive
judgment of all nations has already condemned us: England
stands isolated — — —

Do you recollect our *"drifting* into the war against Russia?"
We had almost come to the same chance against our only brother-
nation—and this would have been the first Chapter of a "Decline
of the British Empire."—I believe we have to thank our most
worthy Queen Victoria for seizing the helm at the last extremity,
and thus saving our country. You say H. M. thinks "German"
in the Schleswigholstein case? I hope the time will soon arrive
where you'll see that *German* in this case is synonymous with
thinking *justly* and *honourably*—therefore by no means *un*-english
I trust. Meanwhile methinks I see an additional ground for
H. Majesty's widows-weeds, for the Genius of England has occasion
to mourn over most imminent Dangers impending.

England is actually adrift — —. Are those boasted new iron-

and ungrateful self-destructive blindness of a Denmark! An Englishman couldn't
bring himself to believe such a thing;- sooner than that you allowed yourselves to
be duped by the most ridiculous, not arguments, nay, nursery-stories, such as that
the Germans (notwithstanding all their conscientious good-faith and active dis-
interested aid for every cause of freedom-even when at their own cost, as in
Hungary) were transformed over night into a gang of cowardly drunken brigands!
The Danes were very active in your papers to construe the affair in their way—
a most curious sample of which appeared in the *Times* of 22nd March. The Germans neglected this, depending upon their good cause; and you did not take the
trouble of translating and studying their learned explanations. Even the gross
contradictions of your own Ministry did not open your eyes; for vaccillating by
turns between every extreme, during the Crimean war they actually held out to
Germany the acknowledgment of her full rights, to induce co-operation.

casings disturbing the compasses of our old "Heart-of-oak?" The Representatives of our nation are discovering the veerings of convenience which jerk us about fearfully on troubled seas—but they have not discovered correction. Where are the secure bearings of a firm principle to guide us into port!—

Dangers?—Coming events casting their shadows—. Refer to the commencement of those gigantic Continental-wars in the beginning of our century, and you'll find that events were decided· beforehand as soon as Napoleon succeeded to break up the union of Germany (by gaining over, "under his protection," the Rhenish Secessionary-League). By the aid of these German small states, and by further splitting the two German Great-powers among themselves, he threw down disunited Austria as well as Prussia. N. used German soldiers in Spain, and conquered Russia by strong aid of the same (at least 80,000 Germans perished in that campaign). It is not difficult to prove that *the awful growth of those wars*—for which even at this day every Englishman has to pay heavy taxes—*was caused by the broken-up state of Germany.* Alas, this cancer has been propagated, and continues to be the fundamental cause of the present peril. Most alarmingly similar is the actual position of Germany now, to that which foretold the hurricane then! The same three divisions are fermenting. In case the rights of Schleswigholstein were abandoned once more, with the present overruling of Austria and Prussia, rebuffed by England: it is very much to be apprehended that the smaller states' Governments would seek "protection" once more from France! Austria would probably soon withdraw - then how could Prussia alone, internally divided, outlive the crisis? (The last days have already commenced to unveil direct proofs for my apprehensions.) A renewal of the Holy Alliance may be less probable, yet the vicissitudes of great struggles may bring on unexpected things - probably not to our taste.

To word the situation concisely: a renewed suppression of that small Schleswigholstein would probably be punished by a general war of even more awful dimensions than the last;—and can you remain in doubt, where the ultimate blow would fall?!—

These reflections have led to an issue very different from that

blustering Threat of war (and which I suppose to be adjourned *ad infinitum,* or ceded to discussion in some other house). The first Theme for contemplation ought to be: **How can England make good past Errors;—is it possible yet to avert impending Calamities, and how?!**—
I believe that redress and rescue *are* still possible, provided every Englishman does his Duty promptly. The first step must be, to reform that deplorable ignorance of facts, which is our only sorry excuse. Those narrow-sighted speculations and jealousies, which no doubt lurk underneath and distract our straight-forward course, will then soon be replaced by a bright horizon, and we shall steer clear once more.

Humanity directs *our first attention* to

Denmark,

where there are festering wounds to be healed—which, perhaps, *we* might have prevented. I can appreciate the motives of Mr. Parson and of that valiant Irish "Cent-Gardes" gentleman, but very different ways and means must be sought!

The time is not far remote when—by peaceful competition—German influence stood high in Copenhagen; nor was this anywise unnatural or injurious, but very much the contrary. It was an unfortunate undertaking to reverse this by force, in consequence of the Eider-Dane agitation which has gradually possessed the overwhelming majority of the people. Denmark has, however, deliberately decided her own doom long ago, and must bide the consequences now. Yet has she only lost something that never belonged to her: S.-H. was only a temporary trust to the person of the Kings of Denmark.

The newest scenes of the Drama are:—A challenge from Denmark to all Germany, by seizing her ships, &c., without being at war; and a refusal of the Armistice offered on the 7th March on more than favourable terms. Thus seeing, that Fanaticism * still continues a war, which can only lead to self-destruction: it becomes

---

* As an answer due to those incorrect Accusations of Germany, I feel a strong temptation to give some most striking proofs for the fanatic excesses of their enemies: yet I desist, because it is my aim to put down passions, to promote cool insight.

an urgent necessity to put a stop. *Immoderate ambition* is the old mortal wound of Denmark. And Schleswigholstein had become another unhealable one; if it were coerced back, this wound would become deadly.

If one part of the monies which were to have been worse than wasted by an English armament, were offered in the shape of a railway for neglected Jutland, or so, that would be *real* friendship. The query, how to appease the excess of excitement, is a very difficult one. You may find fault with the particular cure (a *coup d'état*) proposed by Mr. von Bismarck; but his assertion respecting the evil is right enough: a confirmation of this is the party-pro-gramme of Chamberlain Major Dinesen in Copenhagen.

You sympathise with the new King?--Although I protest against any nation being sacrificed for dynastic family-politics, yet even on this head I can communicate what will take many Englishmen by surprise: By legal inheritance the Landgravine Charlotte of Hesse would now be Queen of Denmark!—the Crown was only a chance acquisition for King Christian—and a *thorny* one I believe. The noble Uncle of our Queen has voluntarily offered resignation at the option of his people—although the Belgian crown is worth more—and he does *not* enjoy that extra-comfort of seeing his daughter a future Queen of England. And as respects our Princess Alexandra—since she feels happy in her own new lot, being a Schleswigholstein Lady herself by blood, name, and birth,—she should generously rejoice to behold her noble little home-country rendered equally happy, through a change of lot likewise. Germany would, I'm sure, embrace the first opportunity to forgive and forget, and to renew its old kindness to Denmark. If you could only see how nobly the Danish prisoners and wounded are cared for; how Danish bravery and de Meza are acknowledged; how dignified are even the witty publications and popular songs: then would you discover a remarkable contrast.

Some Danish voices appear to be adopting a milder tone, but the task of appeasing will remain difficult so long as the passions continue to be stimulated from without. Should Denmark ask for a better lot than Switzerland, in her secure neutrality? Or look at Holland, after having lost her legal possession of Belgium, but through the noble energy of King and people more happy now than previously—could not Denmark do the same? The most natural and happy solution, however, would probably be a reunion with Norway. Not that Sweden should be deprived of a trust so honourably fulfilled, but by carrying out what is said to have been the late King of D.'s ideal, viz. *a Union,* under the sceptre of the Swedish King, *of all the kindred Scandinavians.*—

This wise and legitimate "Scandinavian" Movement is another ominous proof of the harmonious **Spirit of the age.** To understand same it is necessary first to grasp the fundamental key, viz., *the present insurmountable Tendency of the various nations of Europe, to consolidate outwardly their Nationality,** as well as *to fix a new internal Organisation adequate to the advancement of inward Maturity at which they have arrived.* The presentiment of Napoleon I. is being verified under this modification, that the renewed forms of Government are not Republican, but only *the general adoption of that peculiarly English pattern,* by which every people will come to a healthy Self-action, and which at same time will open a new era of happiness for the Kings.

To attempt stopping the Spirit of the times could only be compared to a scheme for filling up the crater of Mount Vesuvius, imagining thus to stop eruptions and earthquakes.—

Closing the general Survey of pending Difficulties, further proofs have to be supplied, why the present disorganisation of the very Heart of Europe (*i. e.* Germany) entails the greatest danger on the whole of Europe, and why Germany urgently needs the most radical cure of all. This case is complicate and difficult, I grant, but it must acquire an importance and an attraction of which you have no conception now, the moment you gain ʼan insight into that noble

German Nation

itsself, which very idea is a riddle to most Englishmen, who know only Prussia, Hanover, Hamburg, &c.

---

* Of course, a renewed independence of, for example, the "Welsh nationality" would be as little advisable as an independence of the component parts of Austria, or as a mutilation of Schleswig-Holstein and Germany.

I shall be quite brief in my attempt of a sketch, impressing the more strongly an *attentive* perusal; and in the face of an existing estrangement (?) I feel bound to declare, that, so soon as you get to know the truth, it will become a moral impossibility for every fairthinking Englishman to persist in an unjust *enmity*. I can assure you, from my own long experience, that the Germans possess a great inward Superiority—I must give such Testimony with the warmest satisfaction; and I cannot repeat too often the conviction, that our own specific English interests will be largely benefitted by the reconstruction of the German Empire.

Indeed, Germany has something *more* to offer than *Sauerkraut*, music, and sausages, than cheap living, Little Princes, and good customers for our manufactures; or than that which Mr. Mayhew is said to have imparted. It causes an ugly impression, it is true, that part of the Germans among you betray an offensive national indifference; it is a pity that Englishmen travel with too much of the "*Cives romanus sum;*" it is unfortunate that our papers are full of anything else, save those mighty "Foreshadowings" in Germany, which they call phantastic day-dreams. But what shall be said to this, that from the highest platform of England a *regeneration* is denounced as "selfishness and revolutionism," which is simply *the utmost practical Necessity* for Germany!!

In this communication respecting Germany I shall, however, choose the guidance of an Authority, who by gigantic universality of mind was so much exalted above national bias, that he was generally rather severe upon his own country, and is censured by most Germans on this account. The following words have been spoken by the immortal writer of "Faust":— *

"I have often experienced a bitter pang, when I meditated on the present position of the German people, which in its individual members is so worthy of regard, and yet as a nation in such a miserable state. A comparison of the German nation to others excites painful sensations, which I strive to overcome in every possible way. For this reason, because the sciences and arts (in which the German nation is known to possess its only particular Empire) soon become the property of all the world, and in them the boundaries of nationality are made to disappear; the consolation that they afford is only of a passive nature, and can in no wise make up for the proud consciousness which you enjoy if you are one of a great and strong nation, that is both admired and feared."

---

* Our Lewis has gained the prize—awarded by Germany—of having written the very best biography of that "great and good" *Göthe*. My quotation dates some 40 years back; how much more energetic it would have sounded now!

A Nation which at its very entrance into history was so promising that a great Roman (Tacitus in his *Germania*) described it, in order to set up a model for his own countrymen, and which actually became successor to the Roman Empire—think back only of the majesty of Charlemagne, and of the colonisation of England—such a nation fell into misfortunes to a degree that from it the "blind Hessians" were once purchased, and that, Ahasverus-like, its citizens still roam abroad neglected, good enough at this very moment to have furnished 100,000 of the best soldiers for fighting out the American war. Searching into the fundamental errors, which did most to entail so long a prostration, the history of Germany (which is one of extraordinary interest) discovers an excess of liberty and rivalry between the manifold tribes (provinces) and ambitious conquests in Italy—which brought on the further consequence that the northern provinces, including S.-Holstein, were neglected. This tenure of Italy (the alluring Legacy to Austria) did in its turn gradually subjugate the German nation and Emperors under the yoke of the Roman catholic Church—thus planting the seeds of the wars of Reformation. *These Civil-wars were the cause of the long prostration of Germany,* the evil consequences of which reach down to the present day. G. became the arena of the hosts of all Europe, unspeakable destruction ensued, and the Empire was virtually broken up then, since the protestant half was made inimical to the southern half (where Catholicism was forcibly re-introduced) and to its own catholic Emperors. It is thus that Germany has purchased, by a sacrifice of herself, the spiritual liberty now enjoyed by all Europe—while Europe grudges the restoration of Germany! Centuries of gradual dismemberment followed. Particularly Sweden and France took away parts of the country, &c., &c. The advent of Napoleon only upset the rotten outward form of the old German empire, and the Nation was broken down into its deepest prostration, from which dates *a state of Interregnum* which still continues.

Such deep and long sufferings could not pass without impressing some ugly scars on the German people. They sought and gained a temporary consolation in the highest spheres of mind and heart (and the historians have yet to set forth how even in these, by

Achievements of priceless value for all mankind, they have proved their full greatness). Yet, so long as cut off from *active* develope-ment, the passive Idealism of the Germans resembled an attempt to get fat on a beautiful *painting* of Roastbeef. At last they became what you call *unpractical*, too angelic a self-denial bringing on a despairing Apathy, an indifference to nationality.* Is it not extra-ordinary how strikingly our great Jubilæus has portrayed the type of such unfortunate mental one-sidedness in his "Hamlet?"

The economy of the Almighty is revealed in a remarkable fact: the sufferings of one member affect all others sufficiently to induce their active assistance. The sufferings of so important a member of Europe as Germany continue to jeopardise the peace and well-being of all others. Germany still offers a permanent invitation for short-sighted schemes to the Ambitions and Designing. It is not so difficult to explain why Germany is permanently endangered by the largest and most consolidated nations being right upon it. For not only is Germany cut up into numerous fragments, which absorb strength and wealth out of proportion; but these sovereign subdivisions again neutralise each other by continual jealousies and separatist policy. Then consider that the old religious contrasts are greatly reduced but not removed, that immense Armies are often used as police-forces against the people themselves—and that the latter, which is the worst of all, have scarcely any say in their own affairs.—Are you aware, for example, that Russia has already succeeded in binding almost every German Dynasty

* I must here insert another Justification, so eloquent and graphic in favour of the German cause of Schleswigholstein that it may convince even the most doubt-ing. 'T is the case of

Lauenburg,

that province of Germany which has been most recently diplomatised into foreign jurisdiction. Now the Danes have in this case some *negative* merits to show up; they have left intact the greater part of the Constitution (which is as independent as that of S.-H.). The splendid ducal Domains of Lauenburg offer a very satisfactory income, so that the small population have to add only a moderate tax-revenue. As to any good influence, however, to be derived from such unnatural connexion, the contrary is evident by a certain stagnation of progress. And yet these German Lauenburgers have in 48 as good as refused fighting against Denmark, and even now a considerable fraction of them would actually have had no objections to con-tinue under such unfortunate foreign rule! quite reminding one of the *bygone* times of S.-Holstein!—In the case of Lauenburg an Indemnification would appear to be just to Denmark.

by family ties? What then could that London Protocol have led to....

"Thus the only thing that can console the German is a faith in the time to come. (So continued Göthe.) I possess this faith as firmly as you do. *Yes, indeed, the German Nation promises a future and is certain to have a future.* To speak with Napoleon, *the destiny of the Germans has not yet been fulfilled.* If their task had been fulfilled, by breaking up the Roman Empire, and by creating as well as organising the new world of the Middle-ages: then they would have gone down long ago. As, however, they have continued to exist, and in such strength as well as ability, I maintain the faith, that they must yet be destined for great things, a Destiny which must be even greater than the gigantic labour of overcoming the Roman Empire and framing anew the Middle-ages, in the same proportion as their present cultivation does exceed the former.".

It was a long and dangerous peregrination through which the Germans had to wend their way, ere they regained the track towards the home of their forefathers. They are approaching thither, they have acquired, through extraordinary experience, an extraordinary inward excellence, strength and ability—but they are not known again, the doors are shut upon them. Perhaps, however, I can bring this nation nearer to your understanding by pointing to a grave that has not long ago closed over a Man and Prince, who gradually gained your acknowledgment of having been almost without his equal—for *he* was a *model-German* in the fullest sense of the word. His deep and true religion, warm humanity, his comprehensive enlightenment, sense of duty, honour and modesty, his domestic qualities: the sum total of all these virtues forms the very Moving-power* which inspires the great German Nation — onward and straight forward to their yet to be fulfilled greater Destiny.

"But (continued Göthe), but a human eye may not foresee the time and occasion, nor may human power accelerate it. Meanwhile, to us as individual Germans there remains the duty of advancing and strengthening the higher developement of the nation, to which every one must contribute according to his talents, inclination, and position; that such higher education may be disseminated in all directions, not only downwards, but also and particularly into the higher spheres, so that the Ger-

* To indicate what "peculiar stuff" the German nation is made of, let me here mention, how during its deepest prostration the impulse of renewed life was prepared by opening the new University of Berlin and by the "League of virtue;" also that the flame was kindled most particularly by a few men, almost divested of state influence, but possessing Authority over *the spirit of the nation*, such as "Father" Arndt, Fichte, Stein, Schleiermacher. This spiritual peculiarity of the Germans, although it cannot be weighed or measured, gives the true standard for calculating their actions. And mind you—as in those new Prussian cannon and Zündnadel-guns —*practical insight* is now much more blended with the strength of German *theory* than half an *Age* ago when S.-Holstein was outwitted.

man nation may not remain behind others, but on *this Field* at least take the lead, so that the mind, instead of being crippled, may be preserved fresh and cheerfully-buoyant, thus being prevented from falling into apathy and pusillanimousness: — in order that, on the contrary, *the German Nation may preserve the capacity to fulfil any grand* Action *which the occasion may demand, when the day of Glory shall dawn.* — "

The "Foreshadowings" of the future....

Unless all signs deceive: this day of Glory is now near at hand.

The first grand Manifestation took place from 1813 to 15, when, side by side with England, the German Nation reconquered its outward independence.

No matter how cruelly the promised internal reorganisation was withheld — for that same Vienna Congress, which cut off Norway from Denmark, attempted as its masterpiece to legalise the dissension of Germany — yet in 1848 the nation stood up again, and thro' a Legislative Parliament (acknowledged by all its Governments) framed a *new* Constitution for the Empire, with the most praiseworthy moderation and consideration for all concerned.

Yet once more the nation was put down — and with it the first liberation of S.-Holstein. Unfortunately England seconded Czar Nicholas in suppressing both.*

But such a reaction of 16 or 50 years is to the developement of a nation only a relapse of frost in spring — which causes the growth to become more robust. And for every discerning friend of humanity it must be highly pleasing to witness the degree of promising health now evinced, so requisite for overcoming the life and death dangers that had so long exercised a winter-like tyranny.

The German movement is going forward with such surity that the late enmity of England has decidedly helped to *forward* it! It is perfectly astonishing to me, that the Germans so little retaliate.

Would *we* give up Kent? — and yet her jewel-County of Schleswigholstein is still more indispensable to Germany.† For this

---

* Even on the Congress of Vienna our English diplomates worked against the German Nation In 1848, however, the same authority is said to have gone so far as to threaten officially, that German War-ships, seen in the German Sea, protecting a violation of Germany — would be treated as Pirates!

† For military men it would be of particular interest to read the striking proofs of a talented U. S officer (Bürstenbinder), which have just appeared. He shows also, how 30,000 Danes have now been, through their favourable positions, almost an equal match for 100,000 Germans. (But this disproportion is said to have been indicated already by Frederick the Great.)

reason has the protection of this German dependency become *the first commencement* of grand Action, of that majestic *Deed* foretold by Göthe. As to *how* the other internal difficulties will be over-·come?, we may entertain good hopes, that the spirit of the nation may enable the Reform to be gradual and not sullied by blood, to which so great an aversion exists here. That acknowledgment of the nation's cause, given by the sovereigns themselves in their last year's Congress, affords strong indications. And one German sovereign has already given a noble example, by voluntarily laying down his crown—how great may be his inward reward!— The papers have been very sharp all along, in discovering weak sides of the King of Prussia; when will they find out that this monarch is now *practically* earning claims for the acknowledgment of the German nation, and that *he has it in his power to do so permanently,* which would never be forgotten....

That unique Cathedral of Cologne is a type of the German nation: After delapidation and neglect—the very design having been lost! —the scaffoldings which hid the immense works are now falling, to unfold sublime beauty. And yet, of those Spires, that are to crown the whole, the foundations only have been so far prepared, centuries ago—they themselves have yet to be built up! When once they arise to the glory of God and Humanity—all Mankind will have reason to rejoice ...

The one most urgent Cure, then, to which I alluded, is *the Restoration of Germany,* the nucleus of Europe, to its ancient legitimate Unity. Thereby will be brought to an end most of those intrigues and speculations which still are a permanent Endangerment of all Europe. Thereby such endangerment will be replaced by a real Equilibrium of the different Powers, by *those peaceful and beneficially mediating Influences* which the German Empire will be enabled then to exchange with the others, as the best Guarantee for mutual Happiness.

———

But if there be one country before others that should rejoice in the Resurrection of the German nation, it is *ours,* because through ties of blood, religion, honour, sympathy and vital interests none other stands so near to us. Let our debt of honour then be made good at once, by a warm acknowledgment of their Justice in a struggle so gallant aud so perilous; let us no longer withhold that hearty Cheer of sympathy which may render *a moral assistance* to such a Nation!*

III.

A NEW INTERNATIONAL CONGRESS—IN LONDON?

"On that point I take a very different opinion, perhaps, from some hon. members. I cannot but regard these Conferences, which failed when coupled with an armistice, but appear to be coming off now without one, to be very much in the nature of a Parliamentary manoeuvre, more for the amusement of the people who live on the banks of the Thames than for the advantage of those in the neighbourhood of the Eider. (Hear.)

Holding that view, dissenting totally from the policy pursued by the noble Lord's Government to the unfortunate inhabitants of the Duchy of Schleswig-Holstein, and believing that these people have been sacrificed by an iniquitous and unjust Treaty conducted by the noble lord at the head of the Government, unless I am moved by other hon. gentlemen (pointing to the Opposition), I do not feel inclined to give way on this occasion. (Hear, hear.)

If I am told by the noble lord that he has very good reason to suppose that by the mystery which is being used he will promote, *not a temporary and patched-up* peace, but *a permanent Peace,* then I think I could conscientiously give way; but as at present advised..."

(Mr. B. Osborne, House of Commons, March 17.)

THE judgment of England seemed for a long time entirely subverted—

You cannot imagine the degree of relief felt by an Englishman who has seen thousandfold proofs for S.-Holstein so long ignored,—to hear at last such a noble Defence ring from the walls of our grand Court of Appeal!—

Mr. Cons.-Gen. Ward of Hamburg was the Precursor of English acknowledgment of S.-Holstein. The Nerve he showed, by facing the former unanimous opposition, might have accomplished a great service to the Country, if he had not been so much defeated by the secreting of part of his dispatches—but he will one day be rewarded by a more independent position.

Sir H. Verney raised the first tame remonstrances; now, however,

---

* Concluded 24th March – the 16th Anniversary of the first Rising of Schleswig-holstein in 1848.

a small but gallant squad has commenced the siege. Their operations will no doubt be difficult, and they will be repulsed in more than one storm. Yet their honour will grow in proportion, and if they recollect the *"Ceterum censeo,"* they surely will live to say with the S.-Holsteiners:--Success must finally be ours!

As to our Press I am sorry I cannot say as much; for although some special Reporters and other authorities have explained the Errors, yet the old tenets are harped over and over again. I must, however, express my special regard to the Gentlemen who represent the *Times* and *Morning Star* on this side, to the latter in particular, for (in date Feb. 11) he avows like a true Englishman—that, after seeing with his own eyes, his old prejudices were entirely exploded, and that he most cheerfully testified to the righteousness of the people of S.-H. and their cause.

Some other movements deserve honourable mention, such as that exemplary Manchester meeting and the Lecture delivered by the Mayor of Gateshead, in person. Also the able explanation of Prof. Müller—which is only strengthened by those lame attacks of *Punch*. Is it not time that such patterns should find a general imitation? That *Danish* meeting in Glasgow stumbled on the right man, by calling upon Mr. C. Blind to speak. His explanations, taken from *reality*, as fresh as the budding spring, will afford a better cure of confirmed errors than the "prepared specimen"—receipts of those *doctored* Blue-Books, which indeed are apt to give the blues.

But the matter is to be taken up, on the 25th April, by a London Conference—although this is greeted with mistrust beforehand.

We see before us a Repetition, with variations, of the Judgment of Salomon. But the Successors of Salomon have turned into modern diplomatic *Doctors*. They have embalmed that still-born creation of 8th May 52; they have made long experiments to galvanise life into it; they have spun out their visitations to Chancery-court longevity. Denmark cries: "Cut up the living child!" Now the true Mother had actually handed over the latter, for a time, to save its life—but has finally "helped herself" and her own offspring. A Conference, to make out whether that "impotent" abor-

tion be not entitled to the inheritance of Schleswig-Holstein—
that was too much for the Paris faculty!, the dangerous query was
raised, as to whether the living true Heir would consent to give
up his birthrights? —

. As if Schleswigholstein had not spoken for itsself, from the
moment the gag was removed, with a very audible *manly* voice!
It is a strange idea to imagine even the possibility of the S.-Hol-
steiners repudiating their independence and German nationality!
Yet if the repetition of ocular demonstration be wished by Europe,
that pleasure might be granted. Who is to give the answer? So
long as the new Constitution of 15th Sep. 48 remains *suspended,*
the present sepresentative-bodies are the two separate Diets
(Estates). That of Schleswig was, if I recollect right, dissolved by
the Danes not very long ago, because its majority opposed the
Danish inroads—although through their powerful influences the
Elections had been sadly crippled, packed and perverted. If you
want to know what was its *normal* opinion, then examine its vote
of 1846, after Denmark had suddenly unmasked the Incorporation-
scheme. *The demand to be admitted into, and protected by the
German Confederation,* was then (with the exception of two members) *voted unanimously.* After the long determined Danish propaganda, the result would naturally be somewhat influenced now in
that direction.—The Holstein Diet, however, has given voice to its
opinions by a Declaration which speaks for the whole "United
State." I intend to embody it in my Supplement—it is to the
point.

What, then, remains to be done by the London Conference but
to consign an abortive parchment to its final place of rest, and to
admit that "the Living have rights!"

———

Now to some *practical* Aspirations. Good consequences are sure
to result finally, even from the sufferings of S.-Holstein, and from
all this bloodshed and danger.

The Premises of the following ideas are, that there exists an eternal
developement in God's world; that, since knowledge—formerly the
privilege of a few—is now disseminated generally, the consequence
will be the peaceable consolidation of nationalities (or groups of

5

such) and of the newly organised constitutional co-operation between rulers and people. And by these new conditions a new international Organ will gradually become indispensible—unless it be only fine talk, that war is to be replaced by a peaceful competition of the nations, unless religion be nothing more than pulpit-oratory, and unless the Millennium, that special wise prediction of Christ, (although it is misunderstood by many) be set aside as a dream of "Idealism."

Our Forefathers had their *Witenagemote* (*Wise* men's *meetings*) to decide on important affairs. Prince Albert has bequeathed to us the high honour of having realised a preparatory union of Industry, by the "World's Fair," which possessed "international jurors." Napoleon deserves great credit for having been the first, officially to propose a European Congress. But the efficacy of such must depend very much on the mode of construction. If grounded on a firm constitutional basis, *i. e.* by the introduction of representatives chosen by the nations themselves; and if the Jurors, far from assuming a direct interference, confine their earnest deliberations to pronouncing wise Counsel: then the institution might soon gain most beneficial influences.

The day of Düppel has thundered over the length and breadth of Europe—the spirit of Frederick the Great is arising in the German nation. *—I have been on the field of battle—*one* thing has struck me even more than the deed itsself, that is, the amiable *Modesty* of the German warriors—so sure a token of further progress. I have witnessed the beaming countenances of the Danish prisoners, who—arriving amidst festive rejoicings over the victory—were astounded to meet a reception most humane, nay *kind.* They

---

* Here is **the Opinion of Garibaldi,** who (similar to England) was first led away to judge by outside appearances. He addressed the German deputations in London, on the 19th April, as follows:—

"Be well assured that it would, now and evermore, be an impossibility for me to sympathise with an oppression of S.-Holstein.

"And as respects your great Nation in general, I harbour a high esteem for its solid good character and its superior developement. I feel confident, that, when you will have gained your Freedom and Unity: everything in Europe will be regulated in a spirit of greater justice. What do I say?—Not alone Europe, nay all over the world the influence of Germany will exercise the most beneficial consequences.

"It is my heart's desire, that you may arrive very speedily at the aim to which you aspire!"

discovered and acknowledged a hundred fold: "the Tydske (Germans) are *good* after all!" * I have seen the temporary crosses erected by the victors "to the *valiant* Danes." On one of them there is an emblem which found a thrilling interpretation in my heart: two hands joined together—the token of *entire reconciliation.*

Shall we resign to France the honour of carrying out such "Ideas," and of taking the lead in a signal Justification of S.-Holstein?—which would be the result of any fair investigation.

Representatives of England, you who may ask without boasting, what other nation enjoys an equal amount of freedom and power? —it is in your power now, to eclipse that great Deed of your Predecessors, which was moved by Wilberforce,: **Create an International Congress,** *in which the People are also represented!* Success must surely attend a wise and persevering endeavour, to reconcile in peace those two hands which belong to the Scandinavian and German nations—noble branches both of the *Germanic* race, which ought never to be opposed in enmity (the persistance of which on the part of the Danes, however valiant, would now become *temerity*). And may the result of the first meeting be an international Treaty, promoting peace and goodwill, thus bringing *new Glory* on the name of London and on our Nation!

Finally, my Countrymen, if anything in this Pamphlet should appear bold, presumptuous, or improbable to you: consider that a 50 years' experience in Germany and perfect independence of position may enable me, at this critical juncture, to give an *opinion.* Politics are no more a prerogative: *A Friend's practical Evidence* – free from flattery to any side— may deserve being weighed, at a time when the speculative Theories of studied diplomates have involved Europe into serious dangers.

"England expects every man to do his duty!"

Your Progress will be watched with the most intent interest, by

a retired old English Merchant.

23rd April, 1864.

---

* What a refutation to those unpardonable accusations of Savageness invented against the Prussians! and for their bombardment of Sonderburg, which the Danes *themselves* had found no ground to complain against!

THE PETITION OF SOME 200 OF THE MOST RE-SPECTABLE CITIZENS OF HADERSLEBEN (the northernmost town of S.-Holstein, 6000 inhabitants) addressed to the German Commissaries now adminis-trating Schleswig, on the 19th February, 1864.

WITH infinite rejoicings, the town of Hadersleben hailed the entrance of the Allied armies. The long depression of mind of the German inhabitants was thereby dispelled; their hearts were filled with joy, and inspired with enthusiasm. The oppression that had existed for so many years, attended with systematic exertions to turn us into Danes; and the most detestable suppression of the German nationality continued without any abatement since Schleswig was delivered over to the Danes at the close of the preceding war. Yet all this oppressive tyranny had not the effect of weakening the just and unchangeable loyalty of the population for their ancient rights and privileges; though whenever we stood up to defend the mutilated remnants of our liberty, we were put down by force, yet have we preserved our consciences clear: and therefore un-measured rejoicings ensued after our armed protectors had entered the country.

The German population of Hadersleben, in giving a warm recep-tion to the high civil Commissaries, most ardently solicit pro-tection against the real and *special enemies of this Country,* that live in its very bosom and never relax their exertions, consisting of the Danish officials, clergymen, and schoolmasters; they request to have these persons removed, whose only endeavours are, and always will be, secretly and openly, by violence as well as by persuasion to make propaganda for the incorporation of the Duchy into Denmark.

It is, no doubt, known to the high Commissaries that at the sorrowful end of the last rising of Schleswig-Holstein, notwithstanding the ancient law that the officials should only be natives of the country, Schleswig was overwhelmed with Danes instead; that the established right, by which all officials must have studied two years at their own country's University of Kiel, was abolished, against all equity and law; and that Danish Judges, administrative officials, clergymen and schoolmasters were installed, partly without any examination of their qualifications, or partly by a sham examination—whilst the native officials were driven into exile.

With this set of officials a new wild and dangerous enemy entered the country. Hitherto the only enemies of the Country were to be found in Denmark, from whence the mob of Copenhagen, assisted by its Danish perverted papers, exercised every nerve to possess themselves of the beautiful Duchy of Schleswig, and to take it unto themselves as a good Booty; yet, in spite of all these intrigues, S. remained true to itself, and clinging firmly to the brother Duchy of Holstein, submitted to its enforced hard fate only with a bleeding heart.

A system of terror now commenced. It did not manifest itself by bloodshed, imprisonment, and other violent measures, thus wa scarcely visible to foreign countries—whilst in the Duchies the German population was aggravated and chicaned in the highest degree by innumerable refined tortures—applied as it were by thousands of stinging needles. Wherever it was possible, the Germans and everything belonging to them were put down; whilst means were invented to afford *the outward semblance of pretexts for an Incorporation* to the raving press of Copenhagen and its inhabitants, who were filled with wild desires for this fine Duchy. Those manifold Danish officials assembled their subalterns and those who became their retainers on account of gain, particularly in the country, and performed the desired demonstrations. Whilst the Germans were denied the permission of publishing a paper, a Danish one was given out here, full of very scurrilous insinuations and denunciations, and it went hand in hand with the corrupted press of the Kingdom, in order to spread the report that the north part of Schleswig had not a more urgent wish than to be united with the Kingdom.

The country folks in particular were baffled by the forementioned manoeuvres practised upon them by fanatical clergymen and school-masters; and hearing continually from the pulpit (!) as well as in private life the same sophisticated arguments, and seeing the same constantly figuring in the only newspaper accessible to them:— their simple minds were at last confused and turned to the belief, that what they saw in print and what was so incessantly repeated to them must have some foundation.

Thus the former unity and concord was put an end to, and re-placed by inward dissension. Under the auspices described, clubs were formed of such men that had been drafted into the Danish army during the last war; also rifle-corps with the avowed inten-tion of counteracting the German population and the privileges of the country; and a Glee-club in which it was expressly forbidden to sing German songs. And recollect that at the same time the very pick of the population (as before mentioned the educated and higher classes, as well in the towns as the large estate-owner in the country, are almost entirely German) were gagged and silenced, first for want of an organ in the press, then by the pro-hibition of petitions and deputations; they had to suffer in silence only upheld by the possibility of a future change; for under the domineering of those Danes, who were invested with the officia powers, and their retainers, it was in vain even to think of redress.

The principal exertion was made *to contaminate the minds of the young.* All the schools, in the villages as well as in the towns, the high schools and grammar schools, were taken possession o either by native Danes. or by such as had studied at the Uni-versity of Copenhagen, or at a Danish seminary. Even the German seminary at Tondern, instituted for the tuition of schoolmasters, was changed into a Danish seminary with Danish teachers. In the country German was not taught at all. The grammar school of the towns, in which from time immemorial the instruction had been in the German language, were forcibly changed into Danish schools, in which German was not even taught as a foreign tongue In the high schools, where it was impossible entirely to abolish

German, it was classed under the denomination of a foreign language, and even then treated with contempt and disestimation by masters who themselves had but an insufficient knowledge of the same, and tought out of school-books which were written in the Danish language by *Danish* authors, consequently replete with orthographic and grammatical errors. Some of the best class-books formerly used were abolished, in order to ingraft, particularly for History and Geography, the works of Eider-Danes, which were *made up* according to that tendency. A planful hatred against every-thing German was inculcated; the pupils were made to sing Danish war-songs in which the country's privileges and its protectors were pulled down. The very name of the Duchy was changed into South-Jutland," to make them believe that they had no country of their own but belonged to Denmark. Danish cockades were in-troduced, the same flags were carried about at frequent excursions and festivities. And any reluctant scholars were injured, hooted down and ill-treated by the Danish scholars in concert with the masters, and found no protection from the latter. And such abuses were continued under the very eyes of the Prussian troops.

It has already been remarked that for the Duchies of Schleswig-Holstein the ancient law exists that all persons who aspire to a spiritual or worldly office must have studied two years at the Kiel University. This law was arbitrarily set aside. The departure and entrance of scholars had been hitherto regulated according to the Usages of the Kiel and other German Universities. This usage was totally changed into the regulation of the University in Copen-hagen and the other Danish schools, so that for this reason the departure of the scholars to Kiel was attended with difficulties.

The *German Latin-school* at Hadersleben (founded by Duke Hans 1567) is through the benefactions of a many town's-persons richly endowed with scholarships, only intended to ease the expenses of the poorer scholars of the town. These scholarships were denied to such as went to Kiel, and only given to those who studied at Copenhagen, even if all the conditions existed which qualified a scholarship, and although on this account many vacancies occurred, or were disposed of to such as were either in possession of several scholarships or not at all in want of the same. Even the scholarships given for several years to students, who, against their will, to procure the same had to make Copenhagen the place of their study, were unjustly withdrawn, in case the students afterwards resumed their studies at Kiel.

This *danifying scheme* for the young was carried out to such proportions, that the High-school at Colding (the nearest town and already on Danish territory) was done away with altogether, in order to draw the scholars from thence here; that by the introduction of all the requisite apparatus and every possible inducement and lure a number of Danish youths were collected to serve as a fit and willing foundation on which to carry out the danifying tendencies. And as not only a many scholars came from abroad, but likewise the number of Danish officials who had been imported all sent their children, and at the same time all German schools were entirely prohibited: what remained to the Hadersleben citizens but to send their children likewise, except those few who had the means of sending their children away to schools in Germany. The Danish system of instruction was altogether deficient, because founded on a system of getting off things only mechanically by heart (whilst the former German masters had cultivated the powers of independent reflection and a real scientific instruction). Particularly the grammar-schools were as bad as conceivable, and this was another lever for driving, would or not, most children into that danified High-school.

The fruits of these machinations found time to mature. Thus in 1861, when it appeared imminent that Germany would take in hand a military correction, a circumstance occurred which created a certain sensation even in Germany, how much more then where the particulars were unknown. Viz.: a number of Schleswig (!) students at Copenhagen in various ostentatious declarations, breathing hatred and destruction against everything German, placed themselves at the disposal of the Danish War-office. Now these were almost without exception the sons of Danes and Danish officials who had emigrated into Schleswig. There were some other countrymen present whose minds were not yet poisoned by the Danish machinations; they refused to sign such declarations and their fate was, that after excessive persecutions they left and went to our own country's university, Kiel, whereupon their endowments, their rights to the benefits of their own town, were cut off, thus bereaving them of almost indispensable assistance.—

To further elucidate the stamp of the Danish Regime in Schleswig, the following details of proceedings in Hadersleben must be added: After a thorough "purification" in the spirit of the Danes, a sort of Dictator (Mr. Hammerich) was installed over the town; for into the hands of one person were merged the offices of Burgomaster, master of police, town-bailiff, and secretary—a man (Schleswiger by birth) who regardlessly pursued his own will, and scorned all consideration. Further all the 3 Magistrates' and 16 Aldermen's offices were filled altogether with real Danes; setting aside the citizens of note, such as possessed an interest for and the qualifications to promote the well-being of the town. The blundering mismanagement at last assumed such dimensions, that the Danes themselves became strongly alarmed; and two vacancies occurring among the Aldermen, the majority in that body resolved to elect substitutes of real capacity. Now as these were only be found among the Germans, they indicated 6 German Citizens, from whom by law the Magistrates ought to have selected 2. The Danish Officials, however, arbitrarily annulled the entire election; by means of every imaginable outward influence and terrorism their clique installed two new tools of their own.

Speaking of the means used by the Danes, they at one time, against all law and equity, struck 19 of the most distinguished Citizens of H. from the list of voters, and at the same time cut off their right of being elected into the Schleswig Diet. This act of gross violation, which was condemned even by the moderate Danes, caused a fearful excitement throughout the whole country: yet what could we do otherwise than suffer wrongfully in silence.

A small incident on New-year's eve last may supply one of those stubborn facts which render comment superfluous. A number of men of character had met in the first hôtel of the town, and were singing harmless German songs, when a strange hand, which escaped undiscovered, smashed all the windows of the room. On the day following the Burgomaster summoned the Landlady, and after an uncivil delay threatened her by the following argumentation: Since her windows had been smashed, this was a proof for illegal proceedings of her guests; if such a case was to occur once more, he would close her hôtel. *

And as an instance of the degree to which the material interests of the country were sacrificed, the method is detailed by which a great ship-wright from a neighbouring town was prevented from opening a building yard – because Capt. Raben was not a man who denied his nationality. The very simple method by which the Dictator effected his end was, to forbid the removal of a harbour-pile which was entirely superfluous, but an insurmountable obstacle for Mr. R.; and thus the town was deprived of the great benefits which would have resulted otherwise.

But why swell out the particulars, it suffices to conclude by stating that the very street-names, German from time immemorial, were daubed over and replaced by Danish ones, and that even the watchmen had to commence a propaganda by crying the hours in Danish language. The language used at Courts, in administration,

---

* I can add an instance myself, how the gentlemen-farmers of that neighbourhood, at their Clubhôtel-balls, were spied over by policemen, and fined because a cake was ornamented with flowers of the national colours. – If you want something more grave, I could detail to you a long history of the method by which the interests of hundreds were assailed on the Isle of Sylt, by Danish attempts to usurp the inhabitants' private sea-bath rights in favour of a Danish Company.

schools, &c., had been metamorphosed by decree of Might:—and now let any one deny that Hadersleben be a *Danish* town!?

Under such jurisdiction of the town, under such parish officers, under such a Burgomaster, and under such circumstances (of which those quoted are only a few seperate items, since they formed one uninterrupted chain of grievances of nationality) the almost entirely German Citizenship had to live on!

Finally the Petitioners pray for the removal of those illegal Danish officials, assuring that under no other circumstances tranquillity, peace and concord could be restored. At the same time they warn the Commissaries that, if left in the country, an army of Spies would be created out of these officials in the very midst of the German Armies (which petition and warning has been cruelly neglected, but likewise awfully verified and punished on the German soldiers). And further, Petitioners request permission for the establishment of an independent *Danish* newspaper that may enable the Danish country-faulks to gain an insight of the deceit so long practised upon them. "These petitions are for the reinstalment of the chartered rights of our country and for their permanent protection, in order that German language, German spirit and German deeds be restored to their own domain; and that here on the country's northern frontier there may be proved, within a short space of time, how rotten is the structure which Danish lies and deceit have set up—for the breath of liberty will make it crumble into dust in a surprising manner, and Schleswig will then stand with its twin-land Holstein as a united and unanimous country and people, happy to have escaped the yoke of oppression—

Grant this, O Lord!"—

(The Petition, as given above, is in part a verbal translation, partly a strict abbreviation of the facts detailed.)

Supplement No. 2.

OBSERVATIONS OF CHEVALIER BUNSEN, the Prussian Ambassador, handed to Lord Palmerston, June 1850, respecting the Draft for the London Treaty.* (See P. 2 & 15.)

I. A Protocol of this description is perilous, because it sanctions a principle of foreign intervention into the internal affairs of an independent power (in this case the German Confederation).

II. It is unjust and illegal since it sanctions in its introduction a diplomatic idea, which is not based on any European Treaty, or on any other legal act, viz., the Integrity of the Danish monarchy (including Holstein and Lauenburg and possibly even Oldenburg, eventually) and it violates thereby the most incontestabe rights of the German Confederation.

(The integrity of the Danish monarchy is a term invented by Danish writers, who from 1806 to 14 wished to prove that Holstein was only a province of Denmark. From that period this term became the "Schiboleth" of those who from 1818 to 46 strove to give Danish officers and word of command to the federal German Contingents of the Duchies.)

III. Such a proceeding would be contradictory to the office of Mediatorship which Great Britain has undertaken between Germany and Denmark, and which she has continued to exercise until this day. (P. 30.)

IV. The arrangement proposed by Great Britain, France and Russia would authorise these three powers (and each of them) to carry out for ever a kind of Protectorship as well over Germany as likewise over Denmark (similar to that exercised over Greece and Turkey).

V. The present Protocol is not any more applicable to the present state of things, because peace is already concluded between Prussia and Denmark (and will soon be accomplished with all Germany).

(This reminds us that one of the objects advanced in the original draft [Art. III.] was to put an end to the war then going on, in accordance with the wish of the English. —But [continues B.] they do not want absolutistic principles to triumph, and defeat

* The above Document is extracted from a work which has enjoyed the patronage of Prince Albert: a continuous Collection of *the official Documents of the day*, by Prof. Dr. Aegidi and Klauhold.

the principle of intervention; and still less does the English people desire to see such a Protocol become the instrument *or the pretext for a systematic intervention in the internal affairs of other countries, and thus the germ of future complications and wars.)*

VI. The project of this Protocol, far from insuring the pacification of the Duchies, would increase the difficulties in the way, inasmuch as it would probably render Denmark less disposed than ever to make just and indispensable concessions to the Duchies.

(Whenever liberal and generous sentiments exist, there will be sympathies for the sufferings of a population which ranks among the most civilised, respectable and most sincerely constitutional of Europe. In a future time it will be found strange that this population, after having been neglected and ignored by the Diplomates of Europe, the while it felt itself the victim of a revolutionary proceeding—that the same population should be finally crushed by a Protocol signed in London,)

Supplement No. 3.

A PROTEST TO GUARD INTACT THE RIGHTS OF SCHLESWIG-HOLSTEIN ON THE LONDON CONFERENCE OF 25TH APRIL, issued by the Parliament (Estates) of Holstein, 5th April, 1864.

"WE the undersigned deputies of the Holstein Parliament (Diet), at present consisting of 49 members, do solemnly make the following Declaration to a Conference of the European Powers about to assemble in London.

"We hereby lodge a Protest against any and all decisions which may be decreed in said Conference, so far as regards the fate of the Duchies of Schleswig-Holstein, and in particular what concerns the person of the successor to the throne of the said Duchies (vacant by decease of the royal Duke Frederick VII.), without having first heard the voice of the country respecting the right of succession of such successor; but on the contrary we declare that any nomination of such a one, that might be made by the European Powers without having previously councilled the Country, would be non-binding and illegal;

"Before God and Man we declare further by these presents, as the established Right of the Country: that

1) The Duchies of Schleswigholstein are for ever united Countries and indissoluble;

2) The male lineage of the Princes of Oldenburg, according to the line of descent and Primogeniture, is exclusively entitled to the throne;

3) According to that the King of Denmark, Christian IX., has no claim whatever to the throne of the Duchies. because he is exempted from the same by legal Heirs (Agnati) who possess prior claims, whereas the London Treaty of 8th May, as well as the Danish law of succession of 31st July 1853, are in no wise legally binding to the Duchies, the former because foreign powers have no right whatever to dispose of a country not their own, and the latter because the consent of the Schleswig-Holstein Parliament, of the Agnati and of the German Diet is wanting;

4) The rather, the legal claimant among the living princes of the Oldenburg house, after the resignation of his Father, Duke Frederick of S.-Holstein-Sonderburg-Augustenburg, who as Duke Frederick the Eighth of Schleswig-Holstein has declared his readiness to accept the government;

"We have further to proclaim the fact, that the voice of the Country has been expressed, in accordance with same, by numerous representations to the German Diet, as also in Homage-addresses and deputations to the Duke Friedrich VIII., on the part of the S.-H. Equestrian order (nobility). of the University, of the Clergy, of the body of Schoolmasters, of the Towns and Country districts as well of Schleswig as also of Holstein, all giving their unqualified opinion that Duke Friedrich of S.-H.-Sonderburg-Augustenburg is alone their rightful Sovereign, to whom they not only give allegiance, but declare their readiness to defend with their blood and property;

"Finally we most solemnly protest against every arrangement of the European Powers which might attempt to enforce on us, against the will of the Duchies. an unlawful Ruler, as well as against linking us once more by force to the Kingdom of Denmark, from which state by the death of Frederick VII. we are finally seperated, and—we throw upon the Originators of such an arrangement the entire responsibility for the damages and dangers which would unavoidably result therefrom to the well-being and peace not only of our own Country, but also of Germany and of Europe."

(This Protest has been adopted and signed unanimously by the 40 Members present, and forwarded by their Committee to the German Central-government [Diet] and to the Powers.)

Dated Kiel, this 5th day of April, 1864.

As to the vote of Schleswig, see the extract from the Declaration of the Monster-deputation *elected* by the whole Duchy of Schleswig, of 27th March, page 33.

~~~~~~~~~~

A part of the National-song:

Schleswig-Holstein sea-surrounded,

according to the translation of Dr. W. BELL, London.

GUARDIAN, true, at Teuton's Portal,
 Shalt not stand assail'd alone,—
Hark our watchwords clang—the word all
 Germany obeys, as one:
"Union—Troth-pledge—Fatherland!—
Schleswig-Holstein's twin-tied Strand!"

Awful warnings!—days of anguish,
 When the Frenchman, Dane, and Swede
Did *by Germans!* Germans vanquish.
 (Elsass still from Gaul's not freed!)
None shall tear from Fatherland
Schleswig-Holstein's twin-tied Strand!

No! the Dane shall have them never,
 Nor the Czar their Sons enthrall;
Rather will our limbs we sever
 With our bodies build a Wall:
E'er to guard for Fatherland
Schleswig-Holstein's twin-tied Strand!

THE END.

www.ingramcontent.com/pod-product-compliance
Lightning Source LLC
Chambersburg PA
CBHW032044090426
42733CB00030B/655